CORPORATE GOVERNANCE

THE DAVID HUME INSTITUTE

Hume Papers on Public Policy
Vol 3 No 4 Winter 1995

CORPORATE GOVERNANCE

EDINBURGH UNIVERSITY PRESS

© David Hume Institute 1995

Edinburgh University Press
22 George Square, Edinburgh

Typeset in Times New Roman by WestKey Limited,
Falmouth, Cornwall and printed and bound in
Great Britain by Page Bros Limited, Norwich

A CIP record for this book is available from
the British Library

ISBN 0 7486 0859 1

Contents

Contributors

Sir Lewis Robertson CBE FRSE has been Chairman of nine public companies and Chairman or a Member of numerous public bodies.

Sir John Shaw CBE is Deputy Governor of The Bank of Scotland.

Dennis J Farrington is Deputy Secretary and Clerk to the Court at the University of Stirling.

Stefan Szymanski is Senior Lecturer in Economics at Imperial College Management School.

Simon J Clark is Senior Lecturer in Economics at the University of Edinburgh.

Brian G M Main is Professor of Economics at the University of Edinburgh.

Foreword

In the Autumn of 1993, The David Hume Institute published an issue of *Hume Papers on Public Policy* entitled 'Universities, Corporate Governance, Deregulation'. Since then, the Greenbury Committee and the Nolan Committee have ensured that corporate governance retains a high level of public interest. The present issue returns to this theme and covers aspects of corporate governance in both the public and private sectors. It also addresses governance issues as they affect the determination of top executive pay.

Sir Lewis Robertson, in a paper based on a lecture recently given in Australia, provides a view of recent developments in corporate governance from the perspective of an experienced senior executive and corporate rescue specialist. After commenting on a comprehensive range of governance topics, including the role of non-executives on the board, the desirability of a separate CEO and Chairman, the efficacy of two-tier boards, and the importance of the nominations process, Sir Lewis raises an often neglected consideration, namely compliance costs. Auditors have adopted a rather prescriptive approach to compliance verification in terms of Cadbury and other codes – an approach spurred in no small part out of concern for their own personal liability. This approach has engendered checklists, guidelines, and standards that have both threatened transparency and driven audit costs ever upwards. For large companies this is an uncomfortable development, but for the smaller firm it assumes a serious proportion. In fact, as Sir Lewis emphasises, recent efforts to design codes of corporate governance seem to have overlooked the problems smaller companies experience in complying with such regulations.

Discussion of the principles of good governance has recently been extended to the public sector through the deliberations of the Nolan Committee. Sir John Shaw provides an overview of the similarities and differences that exist between the public and private sectors in terms of notions of governance and accountability. Such clarification is particularly timely given the upsurge in collaborative activity between the public and private sector, for example, under the auspices of the Private Finance Initiative (PFI). Sir John highlights two key characteristics that distinguish the public from the private sector. They are 'non-financial accountability', arising from the difficulty in quantifying output in financial terms, and 'strictly defined accountability', whereby the objective is narrowly constrained and strictly defined with no flexibility in the application of surplus resources released by economy, efficiency or effectiveness. On the other hand, the issue of going concern, while familiar in the private sector, translates less easily to the public sector with inevitable uncertainty over future funding and its inflexibility in terms of accumulating reserves. The tight limits placed on executive discretion in the public sector can lead to a clash of cultures when agents of the private and public sectors meet to collaborate in joint ventures such as the PFI.

A detailed example of governance problems in the public sector is provided by Dennis Farrington who discusses the state of management in UK universities. He demonstrates how far universities have moved from the traditional view of management by consensus – still widely, if erroneously, believed to apply. Recent organisational reforms of the funding system, the increase in the number of universities, and the redefined nature of academic tenure have turned universities in the direction of being customer oriented businesses. A range of possible models of the role of governing bodies in universities is examined. The analogy with boards of private companies is rejected in favour of a model that is closer to that applying in NHS Trusts. The model for university governing bodies favoured by Farrington claims to place power in the hands of the staff as stakeholders through dominant representation on the governing body, albeit with the input of a small number of non-executives.

One of the most obvious measures taken to suggest slack corporate governance, as seen by the general public, is the high level of top executive remuneration. To date, this attention has primarily focused on private sector companies, but prompted by the Nolan Committee looks set to encompass the public sector in the near future. One common response by executives when criticised regarding the level of their pay is to appeal to the level of salaries paid to football stars or other entertainers. The paper by Szymanski uses the football star analogy as a means of comparing and contrasting the practices and procedures in these two labour markets, namely the market for top executives and the market for professional football players. Particular emphasis is placed on notions of fairness as measured in three senses – procedural, distributional, and market efficiency. The results of these comparisons are claimed to be startling. Professional footballers have moved, over the last 30 years, from a world in which there was little efficiency or procedural fairness to one in which there is a great deal of both. It is argued that executives have been subjected to a dramatic increase in procedural fairness (Cadbury and Greenbury) but with no guaranteed impact on efficiency, owing to a lack of transparency concerning the relative talents of the executives in question. The resulting situation is portrayed as one where a public perception of executive self-dealing can arise. Szymanski offers a solution whereby groups of similar companies should form salary clubs under which a supra-company committee of independent members would determine the 'going rate' of remuneration for boards in their group, while leaving the detailed design of individual director pay and pay structure within each board to the deliberation of each company's Remuneration Committee.

In the final paper of the collection, Clark and Main look at the determination of the structure of top executive pay. The design of incentive pay offers a way in which the difficult process of governance through a company's senior management can be made easier by aligning the incentives of the executive with those of the principals in the company. This is no more than payment-by-results raised to the level of the boardroom. Until recently, executive share option schemes have been a very popular way of achieving this. But certain widespread misconceptions regarding how share options operate and a number of well publicised individual cases of seemingly excessive gains being realised through these schemes have combined to produce a marked hostility towards executive share options. Furthermore, the restrictive regulatory environment placed on the operation of executive share option schemes by institutions such as the Association of British Insurers, the effective withdrawal in July 1995 of tax-benefits associated with these schemes, and the generally discouraging stance adopted by the Greenbury Committee have all combined to incline boards to look to alternative forms of long-term incentive scheme. Clark and Main explain in some detail the strong advantages of share option schemes – in particular, the very high reward (punishment) delivered for good (bad) performance per £ of the executive's forgone salary tied up in share options. Executive share options also ensure an exceptionally strong degree of insulation from the social influence that abounds in small groups (no less boardrooms) and tends to influence decision making (such as bonus determination). Clark and Main make a strong plea for a more vigorous use of share options in designing executive remuneration contracts, while arguing that such a move needs to be accompanied by a more explicit reporting by companies of the values involved in the award of all long term bonus schemes, including executive share options.

The David Hume Institute is pleased to publish this timely collection of papers on a subject of considerable importance but must stress, as usual, that the views expressed in these papers are those of the authors alone, and that publication does not commit The David Hume Institute to any of the views put forward here.

Hector L MacQueen and Brian G M Main
Directors
The David Hume Institute

Corporate Governance: the lessons of recent British experience

Sir Lewis Robertson

This paper is derived from a lecture recently delivered in Australia; some references to Australian circumstances have been retained to give context and to explain the sometimes simplified treatment of recent UK developments.

Introduction

For the past twenty-five years, except for a five-year interlude in the public service, my profession has been the rescuing of companies in trouble. My job has been to recover and repay borrowings (mostly bank borrowings), to retrieve as much value as possible for shareholders, and to preserve the entity. I am glad to say that in each successive rescue the banks have been fully repaid (often to their surprise); and in every case save one the rescued company is still, today, up and running, out of recovery and performing for its shareholders.

This has been strenuous but interesting and varied. The range of activities has been very wide, from golf clubs to heavy muck-shifting to meat, from casinos to storefitting to fine printing . . . and many others. And as can be imagined, in personally tackling these companies, as well as studying and advising on over a hundred more, I have seen pretty well everything there is to see in the way of bad management and bad corporate governance.

The debate – indeed, debates in the UK

For three years and more in the UK there has been much public concern about corporate governance – boards of directors, corporate controls and so on and a great deal of media discussion, much of it very superficial. The concern was in its origins reasonable and sensible enough, fuelled by a number of very prominent, spectacular cases: Maxwell, Polly Peck, Bank of Credit & Commerce International and others, and recently Barings. These disasters happened; were they caused by feeble boards, weak controls and defective financial reporting? Are there rules, guidelines or attitudes that can be put in place to prevent the next series of corporate disasters from happening? In what follows I offer a look at what has been proposed in the UK, and make some observations on what might or might not, should or should not be done about boards and more generally about regulation, in Australia or elsewhere.

Superimposed on the – as I say, generally reasonable – debate on governance, the area covered by the Cadbury Report (1992), there has more recently developed a *furore* over boardroom pay, share options and so on. In one sector, the privatised utilities, there is substance in this, but across industry as a whole it is less reasonable, more emotional, and very much fed by the media, for whom the earnings of footballers and pop stars are matters for admiration and approval, whilst the (usually far smaller) earnings of the chairmen or chief executives of major companies are pilloried and made the objects of silly personal comment and whipped-up envy. I shall deal separately with this issue, which has recently been the subject of the Greenbury Report (1995), named after the chairman of the committee that recently reported on directors' pay and related issues.

And both the 'governance' and the 'boardroom pay' debates (which overlap and intertwine) have coincided with and are blurred by a few cases of questionable propriety on the part of MPs and other politicians. Because of all these together a large, damaging degree of cynicism, even contempt, has got into the public mind, and it will take a lot of time and patient effort to restore a sense of proportion. This cynicism or contempt is not good for industry, not good for business, and not good for the economy; and anything that can be done to avoid creating or fuelling such a public mind must be worth doing.

What we must not lose

Behind all questions of boards, of management, of governance, is one key issue: business will only succeed if it is led by people who *drive*; drive their companies, drive their team, drive themselves. And whatever we do, or say, or prescribe, or regulate, we have to leave room for the driver – the entrepreneur – to operate. Any board set-up, any board and management relationship – for that matter, any chairman and chief executive relationship – has to encourage enterprise, initiative and ideas. There has to be enough questioning, enough accounting, enough challenge to unearth possible problems; but whatever the system is, it has to not confine, not discourage, not cramp the growth-minded. The balance between dictators and ditherers, management scope and management sleaze is not easy to strike, but we have to try.

The board

Separation of functions

The structure and workings of boards of directors need to be thought through in this light. It is accepted that there should generally be a separation of chairman and chief executive. But I believe that there will be particular phases when one individual needs to fill both roles – phases in the growth of an enterprise, in the development of the entrepreneur himself and, I would add from long personal experience, in the early stages of corporate recovery. In these cases the counterbalance (and a counterbalance is important and necessary) is a good external, non-executive boardroom element, independent, experienced, sympathetic to what the entrepreneur is attempting but weighty enough to civilly, rationally ask the sometimes penetrating questions.

Non-executives – many, few, enough?

In any board, maybe with some exceptions in the very smallest private companies, there certainly should be non-executives; and there must be enough of them, both in weight and in number, to influence management, to debate things among themselves, to bring various viewpoints to bear on company policy. The Cadbury Code of Best Practice (1992,1.3) states that:

> The board should include non-executive directors of sufficient calibre and number for their views to carry significant weight in the board's decisions.

This view is further particularised in Cadbury to suggest a minimum of three non-executives of whom at least two should be independent in the sense of being free of any business relationship with the company.

Except in insurance, banking and a few other areas, non-executives in the UK are seldom in a majority, and personally I do not think that this is essential; questions of majority and minority only come up if the board actually divides and votes, and this should not happen save exceptionally. If the non-executives are strong, experienced people they will influence things, majority or no majority. I believe that on a public company board of, say, seven or more directors there should be not less than three truly independent non-executives plus a separate chairman; and if the chairman is, exceptionally, also the chief executive then the non-executive element should be further strengthened, probably by the appointment of a deputy chairman from among them and certainly with good access to information and to independent advice.

What exactly are the non-executives supposed to do? Are they policemen, or policy men, or passengers? There is a real danger, sharpened by the current tendency to try to regulate or legislate to cover everything, that they can drift into being policemen, or can appear to management to be so. To avoid this it is important that the chairman handles the board, non-executives and management alike, so that the feeling of 'them and us' is contained and minimised. This needs a lot of both tact and firmness. The non-executives' job is to support management but also to question it; to get explanations for anything that looks odd or worrying, but not to fuss over detail; and to contribute to policy debate, whilst recognising that in most companies policy is formed in the mind of the chief executive, or certainly has to be fully adopted by him; policy cannot be imposed on management. As to the last possibility, that a non-executive can be merely a passenger, there are no doubt still a few around who act in that way (or rather, fail to act); but they are nowadays certainly a minority, and the load of responsibility imposed by, among others, the Cadbury and

Greenbury Codes and the listing requirements of the London Stock Exchange increasingly enforces an active role.

Two tiers – or many tears

Executives here, non-executives there; executives do this, non-executives do that; does all this amount to a two-tier board? Most – not quite all – of my UK opposite numbers regard the idea of a two-tier board at least with misgivings and more often with outright disapproval. In part this is because when it was floated earlier in the UK by the Bullock Report (1977) it had political overtones, and was put forward as a means of securing worker representation (or probably trade union representation) at board level; in part the dislike (in the UK) probably stems from mistrust of 'continental European' ideas.

I myself do not share this negative attitude, partly because I have worked with people and companies in other countries. In Scandinavia for instance, where two-tier boards are the norm, the senior or supervisory board does not involve any trade union representation, but is a sort of 'council of elders' to which are referred (for examination, comment or review) major policy moves, major items of capital expenditure and, most important, the long-term development and promotion of senior management. I do not believe that this is a bad arrangement; on the contrary, I reckon that a management board is likely to take more care in formulating its proposals (for instance, in major capital expenditure or in acquisitions) if it knows that it has to persuade and satisfy the 'council of elders' themselves usually with long experience of the particular business and a strong base in business outside.

It can also be argued that the way things are going, especially with the regulations and requirements laid upon non-executives, all directors are in reality no longer entirely alike in their duties and responsibilities (as UK law reckons them to be, as in Gower (1992, p.160)), but instead that the non-executives, with the regulatory duties laid upon them, are becoming a separate tier without knowing it.

Non-executives – the search

So we need non-executives; in fact, if we are to staff up all boards to the numbers recommended, we need a lot of non-executive directors. The finding and appointing of all directors, executive as well as non-executive, has become and is still becoming a more careful, professional business than it used to be, and the days of the chairman's thinking round his own circle of friends and acquaintances for a likely non-executive director are passing. Internally the company should define its arrangements for appointments, and some form of nominations committee, composed heavily of non-executives, is becoming usual. The Cadbury Code (1992, 2.4) requires that selection be 'through a formal process', and that this 'should be a matter for the whole board'. Externally there are in the UK specialist databases of available non-executive director candidates, and a lot of skill has been created in matching people and boards. There is also an increasing use of headhunters; these are now pretty well the norm for senior full-time executive jobs, but only a few UK firms have developed a focused approach to non-executive appointments.

Women – we need them

A special issue is the wish, and the need, to get more women into boardrooms. They are, in the UK, still a tiny minority, and this in spite of some real pressure on companies to move in this direction. Chairmen and boards still tend to want women directors with pretty much the same kind of experience as the men themselves have, and this results in very few women being seen as eligible – and those that are, are in danger of being overloaded. I believe that chairmen will have to broaden their ideas and come to terms with the different kind of contribution that women can bring. Many of the most able women have developed their talents in fields other than industry or commerce – perhaps in health care, or higher education – and they therefore do not have the language of management and the board. Perhaps there is room for the Institute of Directors to run special courses, not designed to turn senior women into clones of male directors, but patterned so as to preserve their special outlooks and insights whilst also giving them the language, even the jargon of management.

The Chairman and the Chief Executive

Because I am a corporate rescue man I have had more experience than most people of the chairman and chief executive relationship. In two or three cases I have had a really strong, good contact with the chief executive I have chosen; in one or two cases I have had a very difficult relationship, partly because I tend to choose tough, decisive people, not middle-of-the-roaders. I can certainly say that it is a relationship that needs a lot of thought by both sides, and a lot of openness and frankness, with at least some clearly understood guidelines.

Briefly, the chairman is about running the board effectively and making sure that it works both as governance and as a contribution to policy and growth; and he is about 'patrolling the external frontiers', keeping contact with shareholders (especially institutions), government, the media, and business collectively. He is also about the broad lines of policy (on which he should be a close player alongside the chief executive), the encouragement of growth, and (very important) the development of people – especially but not only the next chief executive. Meanwhile the chief executive is about proposing and executing policy, running the show, framing the budgets and targets, leading the team, delivering the bottom line. There will always be a grey, partly unmapped area between them, and the boundaries can and should flex according to the personal strengths and abilities; what they must both have is respect for the functions of the other, total openness (I say to my chief executives 'I am always totally open with you about everything – until it comes to the preparations for removing *you*!'), and a lot of flexibility.

Regulation

Cadbury

As I have noted, the corporate governance debate has been rolling around now for a few years, stoked at intervals by one or another high-profile collapse or disgrace. The leading UK example is the dramatic failure of the Maxwell empire – though I have to say that I doubt if any amount of 'governance' will cope with outright, totally amoral untruths and sustained misdoing. But we have had several other corporate disasters, Polly Peck, BCCI, in a sense Lloyds of London, lately Barings; and it is understandable (though perhaps simplistic) to find the public crying out that there should be governance arrangements in place such as would have prevented or at least lessened these.

It was as a reflection of this that the Cadbury Committee was set up. Everyone now knows the main lines of the Cadbury Report: separation of chairman and chief executive functions, statements required of directors as to compliance, auditor verification of those statements, remuneration committees, audit committees, a proper proportion of non-executives and so on. The Report was deeply thought through and coherently assembled and was a real step forward in our corporate culture: implementation of it might not catch the blatantly dishonest like Maxwell (and there have been others), but would – and I believe will – improve the honesty and realism of public statements, strengthen the checks and balances within boards and enable shareholders – if, and it can be a big 'if', they use their chances – to look below the glossy surface and see further into 'their' companies.

The Cadbury Report was well received, and there was a surge of support; we all settled down to analyse what we were doing, and how to change it or to re-state it in Cadbury terms. But there was, too, a body of sceptics who disagreed with one or more of the recommendations. It is not surprising that hardbitten bosses who had been combined chairmen and chief executives for a lot of years should cast doubt on the strongly recommended separation of functions. And there was at least one prominent, and successful, company head who had never had a non-executive director, wasn't going to have any, and denounced them as expensive and useless passengers. And a lot of others reckoned, some of them rightly but by no means all, that they were already doing the sort of thing that Cadbury recommended. But the Cadbury recommendations were certainly a positive stride forward, and they were given not teeth exactly, but certainly the power to make themselves felt, because the Stock Exchange made statements of compliance or failure to comply with the Cadbury Code a condition of listing. The Greenbury Code is being given similar force.

Auditors

What was not foreseen, perhaps even by Cadbury, was the extent to which all of this would become an auditors' bonanza, because auditor confirmation was required for virtually every compliance statement (especially regarding the effectiveness of internal controls). Auditors are nowadays nervous of litigation and increasingly apt to shelter behind guidelines issued by their professional institutes instead of relying on judgment, so the whole thing instantly became and has remained rather too mechanical, and decidedly cumbersome and expensive. Cadbury's consequences are only one aspect of a general tendency, in audit and control generally, to over-prescriptiveness, checklists, guidelines and standards, at a big cost in intelligibility and common-sense – and certainly in money.

Smaller companies

Another negative aspect of Cadbury was, I think, a perhaps inevitable failure to tailor requirements for smaller companies as well as for big: once again the sledgehammer is painstakingly fashioned, and brought down with a crash on a butterfly. Many a committee, government or other, has demonstrated how little 'the great and good' know about the small – but still good.

Boardroom pay

The origins of trouble with directors' pay in the UK go back more than twenty years, to the early nineteen seventies, when there was misguided Labour government interference in pay differentials and unwise complicity on industry's part in voluntary pay freezes. These things built up a compression of differentials and a 'coiled spring' effect that was almost bound to cause difficulty when a market economy returned. And all this is now taking place within a pretty general 'envy culture' that has strengthened in recent years – though, as I have said, curiously not applying in the cases of footballers and pop stars.

But the really severe current issue of directors' pay and perquisites was triggered by a number of cases in denationalized utilities – gas, water, electricity – where Government, in privatising, had pitched the offer price low in order to be sure of attracting investors. As a result the executives in place at the time, many of whom had been granted options reflecting their key positions in handling the privatisations rather than their proven managerial abilities, received very rapid and considerable stock option gains. Some of these gains have seemed obviously excessive and unmerited; and public feeling has been sharpened by the fact that these same men were (perhaps rightly) at the same time severely reducing workforce numbers.

All of this led, predictably, to a committee, this time set up by the CBI and chaired by the Chairman of Marks & Spencer, Richard Greenbury. Perhaps in response to public clamour they worked fast, possibly too fast; they brought out a number of quite reasonable recommendations, particularly as to transparency and full disclosure of earnings and of the basis of calculation of incentive payments and so on. Unfortunately they over-simplified as to the taxation of share options, unintentionally hitting middle and lower level staff (an outcome they should have foreseen, and showing again that the great and good have no idea how the small and good live): the fuss that resulted rather obscured the better bits of the committee's work, and we are certainly not at the end of this debate.

Corporate rescue

As I have said, for the last quarter of a century I have been rescuing companies in trouble – serving (though I dislike the expression) as a 'company doctor'. Although this is rather to one side of the central topic of corporate governance there is a relevance, because most rescue is made necessary by failures of governance in one way or another. A full treatment would too much swell this paper, but it is worth giving a few headings as pointers.

Why is rescue needed?

The things that go wrong usually come to a head in the form of a cash crisis; borrowings limits and covenants are breached, lenders and creditors are at risk, the avalanche may suddenly start and prove quite uncontrollable. Behind this situation and causing it will be an array of causes. The board may be badly informed, or weak, and not in control of management nor keeping track of it. Financial controls may be weak, and reporting may be late or poorly followed up. Advisors may not be used, or if consulted may not be heeded. Ill-judged acquisitions may have been made, and allowed to run out of control – a very common cause of trouble. Above all, insufficient heed may – pretty certainly will – have been paid to cash and borrowings, the sharpest indicator.

Priorities for action

So what are the priority tasks of a rescue chairman? First, he must keep the lenders (the banks) in place for long enough to permit the rescue to operate – a complex and difficult task when, as often happens, there are many banks involved, some of them foreign. Second, he must control and sort out the board; its members will be shell-shocked by the approach of disaster, and those that are to remain must be picked up and dusted down and the others got rid of, as considerately as possible. Third, he must evaluate and, if necessary, change management; but this need not always imply a blood-bath, for square pegs can often perform better if dug out of their round holes and put into square ones that suit them. Fourth, he must take necessary and urgent management, policy and structural decisions, as for example in identifying which parts of the company must be sold to gain financial elbow room; but he should not take too many of the non-urgent decisions, because these may be better left to the new chief executive. And last, and arguably most important, he must find and instal the new chief executive – and there is a whole book to be written on that, the essential specification, the choice of headhunter and so on.

The Rescue Chairman's kit

What does the rescue chairman need, in doing these things? Wide experience, to enable him to perceive the common patterns of trouble beneath the superficially particular and individual aspects of a given company. A high degree of confidence and a very strong will, to avoid being deflected by distractions of detail or by conventional thinking. A lot of personal credibility, to retain the confidence of lenders, banks and shareholders. And last but not least, a reasonably strong constitution (for it is a strenuous job) and a very patient and supportive wife.

Conclusion

In the field of regulation, what lessons do I draw from Cadbury and post-Cadbury?

- it is better to achieve consensus on corporate practice than to wait for Government to impose what is likely to be a too rigid structure;
- transparency and disclosure should be the cornerstones;
- institutional investors have to pick up the responsibility for studying 'their' companies and reacting sensibly, patiently but in the end firmly to what greater disclosure enables them to detect and diagnose;
- it is important to scrutinise any draft rules with a view to limiting, so far as possible, the need for expensive and often 'overkill' auditor verification procedures;
- everyone needs to be aware that all of this greatly increases, indeed multiplies, the work expected of non-executives and the responsibility laid upon them;
- whatever body is used to draft new rules, it should be broadly representative, of small as well as large companies.

And, from Greenbury and otherwise, what lessons as to remuneration?

- attempts at direct control of levels of boardroom pay by legislation, even by regulation or by stock exchange sanctions, are ill-advised, almost impossible to draft and bound to cause distortions;
- transparency and disclosure are the way forward on remuneration, as on governance generally;
- there are many alternatives to stock options as means of long-term incentive, and boards should watch for new methods of remuneration and incentive;
- again as with governance, it is important to remember the needs of smaller companies as well as bigger ones.

In all of this, it is necessary to ask whether we have done or are doing enough in these fields? Are we succeeding in tackling the various challenges that must be confronted in the area of corporate governance? Are we successfully educating the public? Have we managed to avoid over-prescriptiveness (which may kill the goose but will fatten the auditor)? What can be done to give entrepreneurs space and freedom whilst maintaining reasonable monitoring? If disclosure and transparency are indeed the right way forward, will institutional shareholders play their part? Are institutions willing – indeed, are they free – to think and act for the long term? Given that the chairman has heavy responsibilities – for the effective manning of the board, for the balance between board and management, and for board information, conduct and focus – can the right people be found to serve? And, crucially, will shareholders support and encourage the chairman in the application of good governance?

Corporate governance is currently in a state of almost continuous review and of flux. There are clear opportunities to create more accountable, open and responsive boards and, equally important, to educate the public and the media on the realities of governance and management. The challenge is to do so without undue damage to the flexibility and effectiveness of those same boards, and without undue bureaucracy and cost, in time as well as in money.

References

Bullock, Lord, 1977. *Report of the Committee of Inquiry on Industrial Democracy*. London: HMSO, Cmnd. 6706.

Cadbury Committee, 1992. *The Financial Aspects of Corporate Governance*. London: Professional Publishing Ltd.

Gower, L.C.B., 1992. *Principles of Modern Company Law*. London: Sweet and Maxwell.

Greenbury, Sir Richard, 1995. *Directors' Remuneration. Report of a study group chaired by Sir Richard Greenbury*. London: Gee Publishing Ltd.

London Stock Exchange, 1995. *The Listing Rules (Yellow Book)*. London: London Stock Exchange, London EC2N 1HP.

Governance and Accountability: public and private sector contrasts

Sir John Shaw

Introduction

In a previous paper[1] about governance in the corporate sector I commented on the Cadbury Report and its Code of Best Practice. The conclusions offered were that the Report had been the basis of much constructive discussion and debate and had contributed to wider and better understanding of the principles involved in private sector corporate governance and accountability. That article offered three broad conclusions:

> Managerial performance and effectiveness is vitally important to securing economic and social benefits; enhanced accountability contributes importantly to ensuring enhanced corporate control which will in turn stimulate better management.

> Individual directors need to accept personal responsibility for the contribution each must make to corporate leadership and to the definition of corporate objectives.

> A two-tier board structure which distinguishes explicitly the different responsibilities of governance from those of management may provide a beneficial framework for governance and accountability.

The principles of good governance have obvious relevance beyond the corporate sector. This paper seeks to extend to the public sector discussion of the Cadbury principles and conclusions in the context of the work of the Committee chaired by Lord Nolan on Standards in Public Life ('The Nolan Committee'). It seems appropriate to explore similarities and differences of public and private sector mechanisms of governance and accountability when there is growing international interest in the creation of partnerships between the public sector and the private sector to bring to fruition various infrastructural projects. This interest is focused in the UK most sharply in the Private Finance Initiative ('P.F.I.').

The Nolan Committee

The establishment of the Nolan Committee was announced in the House of Commons by the Prime Minister in October 1994 and it is now constituted as a standing body whose members are appointed to serve for three years. Its key terms of reference are 'to make recommendations as to any changes in present arrangements which might be required to ensure the highest standards of propriety in public life.'

The Nolan Committee was set up in response to publicly-expressed disquiet about some individual instances of personal behaviour – but not to deal specifically with those instances – as was the earlier, less formal, Cadbury Committee. The concerns which triggered the creation of the Nolan Committee, however, related to the behaviour of members of parliament and others holding public office. As already noted the Nolan Committee reports to the Prime Minister and is a standing committee, the costs of whose work are borne by the public purse. The Cadbury Committee, in contrast, was an *ad hoc* private sector initiative with a limited life.

As was recommended by Cadbury, however, not only has there been an initial review of the impact of its work but a second Committee under the chairmanship of Sir Ronald Hampel has been set up (in late 1995) to consider further development and refinement of the Cadbury Committee's recommendations. And in the meantime, a different *ad hoc* private sector Committee under the chairmanship of Sir Richard Greenbury has considered and issued recommendations about the processes of determining and reporting the remuneration of senior executives of limited companies, particularly that of the most senior members of the Boards of Directors of publicly listed companies. This last Committee is yet another example of an attempt to deal with a politically sensitive public issue by private sector review, and to attempt to achieve the disciplines of regulation by more extensive disclosure. (In the case of Greenbury, very much more extensive and detailed disclosure!)

In its first Report, published in May 1995, the Nolan Committee observes that it . . . 'cannot say conclusively that standards of behaviour in public life have declined. We can say that conduct in public life is more scrutinised than it was in the past . . .' The Committee identifies seven principles of public life as Selflessness, Integrity, Objectivity, Accountability, Openness, Honesty and Leadership. These characteristics of conduct are as appropriate in the private sector as in the public, and are entirely consistent with the argument in the previous paper for members of boards to accept individually personal responsibility for the effectiveness of corporate governance.

The Committee's initial recommendations were addressed to members of parliament, ministers and civil servants, and quangos (non-departmental public bodies and national health service bodies). They dealt largely with questions of propriety – the avoidance of conflict between public responsibilities and personal benefit – but also addressed the issue of transparency of the appointment process for quangos in which government ministers exercise considerable discretion (often suspected of being dispensed as patronage). The approach of the Committee is, on the whole, consistent with the British approach of securing regulation by openness rather than detailed specification. Unlike Cadbury and Greenbury which produced their own model code for the members of boards of limited companies and sought London Stock Exchange support to encourage compliance with detailed procedures, Nolan's approach is to urge the development by various organisations of an appropriate code of conduct. There are echoes in Nolan of the work of Cadbury and Greenbury, particularly in discussion of the desirability of audit committees, nominating committees, and remuneration committees but all in the context of more generalised issues.

The Nolan Committee clearly wants to see the public sector covered by a variety of codes which reflect for specific responsibilities and priorities a consistent pattern of respect for and observance of universal basic principles – the seven principles referred to above.

The public sector

The phrase 'the public sector' is used as shorthand for a wide variety of institutions funded substantially by national and local taxation. It extends from departments of government through local government and its departments to public agencies and non-departmental public bodies. Under recent 'Next Steps' initiatives it extends to various executive authorities including Health Boards and Hospital Trusts in the health sector, School Boards in the educational sector. It will extend to bodies constituted technically as companies limited by guarantee whose major or sole source of funding is derived from public funding, for example, in Scotland, Local Enterprise Companies as agencies for delivering, locally, economic and industrial development and skills training. There are extensive networks of autonomous organisations which receive significant financial support in the form of local and national government funds and as grants made through various 'Councils' which are responsible for distributing public funds. Examples include the performing and other arts organisations funded through the Arts Council of Great Britain and the Scottish Arts Council, and universities and higher education institutions funded through funding councils for England, Scotland and Wales (and further education in England and in Wales – in Scotland this funding is currently dealt with by the Scottish Office directly).

General principles of governance and accountability

The earlier paper, already referred to, argued that governance and accountability were two sides of the same coin. It was contended that their inter-relationship should operate benevolently; good governance will be achieved by those governors who earn the confidence and respect of the governed. That respect of the governed generates and reinforces the authority of the governors and enables them to achieve their goals – goals which must be acceptable to the governed.

The democratic process secures that acceptability by ensuring that those taking decisions, whether parliament, ministers, or civil servants, will always be subject to ultimate control by the electorate. The effectiveness of electoral control will be influenced by the way in which decisions are accounted for and explained. Perceived weakness in the processes and standards of parliamentary or executive decision taking will provoke public disquiet, which in turn will prompt democratic pressure for remedial action. As noted above, the creation of the Nolan Committee and its initial work was provoked by uncertainty about the boundaries of acceptable conduct for those in public life. These boundaries need to be defined, and periodically re-defined, in order to preserve public confidence and electoral respect on which depend both the effectiveness of governance and of its authority to govern. That authority will be rapidly undermined by any sustained loss of confidence. Individual leadership and initiative creates change, but joint action and shared responsibility secure appropriate accountability on which rests confidence in that leadership – and thus the authority to lead. This shared responsibility and shared authority of the governed and those governing is of crucial importance to any system of governance.

Transparency is obviously as important a tool of accountability in the public sector as it is in the private. It is difficult to discern significant philosophical differences between the public sector and the private sector either in the principles of effective governance, or in the principles of effective accountability on which it depends. But there are important differences between the processes appropriate in a politically-driven public sector and a market-driven private sector.

Two characteristics distinguish the public sector delineated in this way from the private sector. These are first, the difficulty of measuring outputs in financial terms, and second, the exercise of ultimate parliamentary control through the responsibilities of individual accounting officers.

Non-financial outputs

Adam Smith believed the notion that an efficiently functioning market within which participants exercised improved choices was perhaps the most effective form of democracy. He put it thus:

> 'The natural effort of every man to better his condition, when suffered to exert itself with freedom of security, is so powerful a principle, that it is alone, and without any assistance, not only capable of carrying on the society to wealth and prosperity, but of surmounting a hundred impertinent obstructions with which the folly of human laws too often encumbers its operations'. (*Wealth of Nations* IV, rb43).

But Smith also acknowledged that there were areas of activity where market imperfection or market failure exists to such an extent that Government 'interference' or action is inevitable and inescapable. The State is required to act to provide benefits sought by the community when the market cannot operate because individual citizens see either no prospect of personal economic gain or inadequate reward in relation to available alternatives, or because the scale of a project exceeds resources readily available through the market.

The provider of public goods and public services – in common with any corporation in the private sector – has to provide information to those who provide the resources for its activities. Priorities of objectives have to be established, choices made about the means by which objectives are to be met, and decisions made about the economy, efficiency and effectiveness with which executives manage the resources made available. That is at least part of the business of governance. Distortions in the provision of such information for decisions, whether in the private or public sectors, will lead to instances of failure of governance.

In contrast with the private sector, where the mechanism of price can be used to secure effective allocation and distribution of resources, the public sector's outputs are characteristically not best measured in terms of financial profit or loss. Because many activities are in the public sector precisely because there is no effective market mechanism to drive the allocation of inputs it is not surprising that measures of outputs are not available in market-oriented financial terms.

Private sector resource will be allocated on the basis of perceptions of potential market-driven reward and success or failure judged by the extent to which these expectations are achieved. In the public sector, although inputs can often be measured financially, resources will be allocated on the basis of politically-determined priorities. Because outputs may not be readily measurable in financial terms judgements about success or failure will be complex. (One might note in passing that privatisation programmes, tendering for private sector provision of public services, and such programmes as the Private Finance Initiative, are all attempts to introduce the disciplines and rewards of financial markets into the public sector).

At the end of the day, the success or otherwise of public sector implementation of policy objectives will have to be judged largely in qualitative terms. In the private sector, business performance will be judged largely in financial terms, reflecting the market-driven decisions of customers, suppliers, employees, and determining, in turn, the decisions of investors and lenders.

The roles of these different economic agents in the private sector clearly define the bases of their judgements. The sharpness of the distinctions of their roles and criteria are not blurred by their interdependence. The realisation of that inter-dependence is reflected in such terms as 'stakeholder' used for example by accountants and economists (and now by politicians!) to express that notion of interaction among participants and between each participant and the business itself. In the public sector the distinction between 'customer' and 'investor' is less clear cut. It is not always clear in publicly-funded activity or service whether the principal role of the State is as provider or as consumer – i.e., as investor or as customer. This complicates further the difficulty of trying to 'synthesise' the measurements and disciplines of the market-driven private sector. And it does not seem to be helpful to suggest that similar convergence of roles of investor and customer is found in mutually-owned organisations in the private sector (e.g., most building societies and some life assurance companies). There is similar difficulty in defining mechanisms of governance and accountability in such mutual organisations.

That uncertainty about relationships between managers and the State – as both surrogate investor and pseudo customer – creates distinctive difficulties for developing clearly understandable mechanisms of governance and accountability in the public sector.

Strictly defined accountability

The second major distinction in the public sector compared with the private sector seems to lie in different perceptions of financial resource.

In the private sector, investors seek financial reward (in profit or interest) commensurate with their perceptions of the risks of total or partial loss of their capital. Investors prioritise their investments among the alternative opportunities available on that basis. Evaluation of the balance between potential risk and reward will be informed by business plans and records of achievement of its prospective managers. The investor exercises free choice in making his investment. Once made, managers have considerable discretion over the precise nature and timing of expenditures to achieve the objectives which attracted investment. (They will, of course, be expected to provide the financial return anticipated and specified by the investor.) As the venture matures, the discretion of the managers will extend to expenditure on new ventures, new activities, and fresh investments all financed by retained profits generated in excess of those required to satisfy the initial investors' expectations of dividend or interest and repayment.

Issues of governance and accountability in the corporate sector therefore include the need to satisfy the investor/proprietor that the manager is exercising his extensive discretion over financial resources honestly and effectively in the long term interests of the investor. The relationship between investor/proprietor and manager is fundamentally one of trust – or at least the expectation of propriety.

A different approach to financial resources in the public sector seems to derive from the realisation that most public funds are not made available to the State voluntarily as the result of personal discretion and decision. Public finance derives in the main from taxation, from coercion. This feeds a view that particular rigour should be applied in defining precisely how money provided involuntarily should be used by the State and in ensuring that it is used efficiently, economically and effectively and only for precisely specified and controlled purposes. Those who control and dispense public funds act as quasi trustees of the interests of all citizens – those who collectively provide the financial resources.

This lofty concept of public responsibility is translated into the practical and sophisticated mechanism of control in the public sector through accounting officers. These constitute links in complete chains through which can be traced individual personal responsibility for ensuring regularity and propriety in dispensing money and for securing value for money as a result of doing so.

The concern with regularity and propriety derives from the detailed regulatory framework within which public sector activities are conducted, (which in turn reflects the importance of securing an appropriate balance between the interests of the community and the individual.) But that focus also acknowledges that the private sector market-based measurements of financial profit (or loss) are not available as indications of relative success (or otherwise) in striking an appropriate balance among the claims of investors, managers, employees, customers, suppliers and the community. The absence of such conventional market relationships and the lack of financial output measures also drives the need for a more explicit search for assurance about the attainment of value for money. While value for money is, obviously, as much sought after in the private sector, it can there be largely be subsumed in other market-related internal and external measures of performance.

Public sector politically-driven decisions, combined with strictly defined relationships and procedures, requires that accounting officers may apply the resources entrusted to them in only very narrowly constrained ways. In stark contrast to managers in the private sector, accounting officers have virtually no discretion in the use of funds – or even, in respect of the 'annuality' of the national budgetary and public expenditure processes, in the precise timing of authorised expenditure. Apart from restricted opportunities to 'vire' - that is adjust expenditure at the level of detailed heading of outlay and at the margin – an accounting officer who achieves 'economy, efficiency and effectiveness' or 'value for money' is denied the private sector reward of discretion over the application of 'savings' or 'surplus funds' generated by his managerial prowess.

Supervision and control over the use of public funds aims to ensure that resources are applied only to achieve defined policy objectives and resources made available but not required are returned to their original source, the general pool of State revenues. Money is spent only for the narrowly-defined purposes for which it has been entrusted to the accounting officer with, of course, an equally strong emphasis on avoiding waste, extravagance, carelessness, incompetence, or dishonesty in the application of funds.

These detailed public sector mechanisms of accountability - reinforced by the activities of the National Audit Office and the parliamentary Public Accounts Committee – do operate effectively to secure these basic objectives. In the context of those objectives, they are more structured and more rigorous than the usual internal control processes of the private sector which have broadly similar objectives. These public sector processes do emphasise very tight limits to executive discretion, and could be characterised as reflecting a relationship of distrust – or at least an expectation of failure!

Public and private partnerships

While quangos – quasi autonomous non-governmental organisations – have been a feature of our public sector landscape for many years, they and their look-alike Non-Departmental Public Bodies ('NDPBs') have become much more numerous in recent years with the creation of 'Next Steps' agencies and the involvement of private citizens in boards and governing bodies of activities hitherto entirely within the public sector.

An obvious difficulty for 'lay' members of such boards is that they are brought within the overall structure of public sector governance with responsibility for contributing to the overall supervision and control of the execution of government policy. But they do not become part of the well-established and rigorous mechanisms of accountability and control just described. The relationship between the designated accounting officer – usually its chief executive – and appointed members of the board is therefore a sensitive and potentially difficult one – and one which is not analogous to those in the private sector. There are procedures designed to protect the interests of the accounting officer by ensuring that he can record formally his dissent from the decisions and instructions of his board. But the exercise of such a right is a 'weapon' like the atomic bomb which would destroy the basis for future development. Exercise of such a 'right' would probably signal the failure of the desirable constructive relationship between the chief executive and his board. It would probably bring the board and/or the accounting officer into conflict with the responsible government minister. Nor is it satisfactory that there is no corresponding process to protect members of the board, whose own 'atomic bomb' would seem to be simply to resign. Obviously, the chairman of the board will feel the consequences in practice of such strains most acutely, and will be most sensitive to the issues in principle.

This relationship between a public sector board and its executive is further complicated by the varying degrees of autonomy in appointment of the chief executive. Regardless of the extent of power over appointment, its terms will have to be compatible with public service scales and conditions.

There is, therefore, a different perception of the responsibilities and the authority of 'lay' members of the board with regard to the 'professional' executive compared with those now commonly understood in the private, corporate sector. Further difficulties in understanding also arise in relation to the extent of board responsibility for setting operating policy, for supervising executive effectiveness, and in relation to responsibilities to advise ministers. The condition that such advice is tendered in private may be a further source of complexity. Differences between public and private sector responsibilities seem, in practice, to be one of the less understood and more difficult aspects for those involved from the private sector in such public sector committees and boards. Misunderstandings about such differences can lead, in extreme cases, to frustration and withdrawal from membership of some best equipped to make an important contribution to governance in the public sector. The Nolan Committee's commentary on procedures for appointment to NDPBs have not yet extended to these complex 'cultural' issues.

Many other 'hybrid' organisations depend solely or substantially on public funding to achieve their objectives. They include arts organisations, educational institutions and learned societies, economic development agencies, and many social welfare organisations with charitable status. These are all examples of partnerships between the public and private sectors, with finance, expertise and managerial talent being provided in different proportions by both sectors. Often such organisations are constituted under the Companies Acts as companies limited by guarantee. That may complicate relationships of governance for board members further by overlaying on the public sector approach to accountability the general responsibilities of directors under company law. At least some of these have been both clarified and others arguably made more onerous by the work of the Cadbury Committee. Examples would include each director's responsibility for ensuring that systems of internal control to safeguard the organisation's assets are created and maintained. There is also now a need to declare explicitly that a going concern basis of accounting is appropriate. And members of the board of a company have to consider whether or not they risk suffering the serious personal consequences of being a director of a company continuing to trade while insolvent.

Issues of 'going concern' and possible 'insolvent trading' are given added point by the annuality of public funding and the consequent lack of certainty – to varying degrees – of adequate future funding. The restriction of public funding to specific purposes, and the inflexibility in the application of 'savings' compounds this difficulty further by making it practically impossible to accumulate reserves out of public funding. (Retentions are, of course, possible from private sector streams of income and funding). By definition, a company limited by guarantee has no subscribed share capital and this difficulty in building up the equivalent of equity capital means the organisation cannot confront the financial risks involved in new ventures or activities. Even more important in current circumstances, equity or quasi equity is needed to confront the financial shock of discontinuing activities no longer relevant, needed or sustainable. Such 'discretionary' resources are essential to permit the implementation of transformation strategies – to move from the present to the future.

If there is any validity in the proposition that the disciplines of public sector financing deny the accumulation of such equity in the form of 'free reserves', this constraint on the ability of a 'hybrid' organisation to re-define its mission, strategy, or activities may well inflict substantial damage on individual institutions, and on whole sectors of activity.

The practical difficulties encountered by those private sector organisations anxious to support and participate in the Public Finance Initiative suggest other areas where public and private sector cultures and precepts collide damagingly. Too often the private sector feels itself caught up in internal wrangling between a potential sponsor department (or among such departments) and the Treasury. Too often there seems a lack of understanding of the private sector financier's need to control his exposure to risk by seeking to recover a significant – if minority – proportion of the total outlay during early years of a project, and probably from a dedicated source of funds. Too often there seems to be a lack of understanding of the importance of contractual arrangements as a basis for reassurance on continuity of activity and cash flow. To the extent that these, and other, difficulties flow from what often appear to be dogmatic practices of public sector funding, such practices need to be re-examined. Their modification could obviously assist the growth of the

Private Finance Initiative. The recent restrictions on Government funding of capital projects is clearly based on an expectation that many of the present obstacles will be removed. It is important that they are.

The fundamental difficulty may lie in the contrast between private and public sector cultures: on the one hand, the free choice exercised in capital markets by the investor, involving extensive executive discretion; on the other, the politically constrained allocation of public funding by the State, associated with very tight control over the executive.

Discussion of the issues is currently stimulated by the work of Cadbury and Hampel and Greenbury Committees from the private sector and Nolan in the public. They are contributing to much wider debate about the philosophy and practices of governance and accountability. From the work of these committees and from the debate they are stimulating should come a better understanding of that philosophy, improved practices, and enhanced understanding of the individual responsibilities of those engaged in the process – and perhaps the transfer into the practices of both the public and private sector the best features of each.

Notes

1. Shaw, J.C., 1993. Governance and Accountability: Corporate Governance. *Hume Papers on Public Policy*, **1**, 20–35.

Universities and Corporate Governance : a model for the future

Dennis J. Farrington

Introduction

As Boyer, Altbach and Whitelaw (1994) conclude, how universities govern themselves remains 'one of the most confusing and tension-ridden issues in higher education.' Less than twenty years ago, Handy (1977) could take the traditional UK universities as the archetypes of his 'organisations of consent', self-governing communities practising what Bargh, Scott and Smith (1995) now describe as 'dignified' rather than 'efficient'governance. Although it may be possible to describe some of the informal processes in universities in terms of collegial interaction, in law universities are controlled by governing bodies[1] the formal role of which is described below.

Fielden and Lockwood (1973) described universities as organisations having corporate responsibilities and possessing power to 'manage' the activities of their members in order to carry out those responsibilities. Any serious suggestion in the 1970s that the traditional universities were 'managed' in the modern sense would have been received with, at the very least, considerable scepticism. If under the dignified veneer there was any base activity of *that* kind it was management *by* consensus, rather than management *of* consensus, the second step in a progression from true collegium to industrial management.

I also look at what is now expected of governing bodies given that after the reforms of 1988–92 a significant proportion of universities openly identify themselves as 'managed institutions' with little or no pretence of collegiality. As a corollary, the number of 'managers', particularly those concerned with the control of financial resources, has reached unprecedented levels in institutions, even in those which still claim elements of collegiality. Whereas it was once reasonably clear that the university was governed by the academics for the academics, with advice and support from sympathetic administrators who were also expected to run the show, it is arguable that now the roles are largely reversed, with universities becoming what Toyne (1991) describes and Welch (1995) derides as 'customer-based accountable businesses.' This transformation from the dignified self-governing community into the efficient accountable business has led to comparisons being drawn between members of governing bodies and company directors and in what follows I attempt to rebut that analogy. Finally, I postulate a model which builds on the best of the dignified and the efficient.

Formal arrangements for governance

If we were to propose a form of governance for universities from scratch we would not, as is often said, 'start from here.' It is not an easy task even to describe succinctly what the current system is and commentaries by, *inter alia*, Fielden and Lockwood (1973), Handy (1977), Morrell (1986) and Hayward (1986) have to be read in their historical context. Since 1992 the arrangements can no longer be described in terms of a simple model of charter and statutes (or, in Scotland and a few English universities, an Act of Parliament and local rules). The instrument of government is now more likely to be an Order of Council made under statutory powers or a Memorandum and Articles of Association. In all cases the effective executive governing body is that variously described as the Council, Court, Board of Governors or Court of Governors, made up of a majority of independent[2] members appointed from outside the university and a minority of staff and student members[3].

England's oldest universities do not have an independent element in their governance, ultimate power residing in bodies elected by the masters, deriving, after several reforms, from the students/masters framework as originally established by acts of the Church and the Crown in medieval times. The last university to be founded in this way was Durham but unlike Oxford and Cambridge it has subsequently acquired independent members in its governing body (Whiting, 1932). When, as a result mainly of local initiatives, colleges began to emerge which would eventually become universities (some like Huddersfield had to wait a very long time!), those who founded them wished to retain some control over their government. This is reflected in Scotland in the formal mechanism for the appointment of the Principal of the University of Edinburgh, originally a 'tounis colledge.'

Ellis (1972) quotes the nineteenth-century educationalist Mark Pattison as saying of Aberystwyth 'The issue [in relation to the establishment of a Council] was whether the College should be managed by those who find the money or by those who receive it.' The oldest English example is the institution which became King's College London, established by a deed of settlement in February 1826 as a joint-stock commercial company. When it became a self-governing chartered corporation in 1829 the role of the independent governors was preserved, with the corporation consisting of perpetual governors holding various offices of state, life governors and proprietors who were the shareholders in the original company. The Council of the College consisted of the perpetual and life governors and others elected from the proprietors (Hearnshaw, 1929).

Hayward (1986) describes how the form of government emerged, and became incorporated into the Privy Council's model clauses for university charters and statutes, in which the responsibility for the finances, property and staffing of universities was vested in the Council (Court in Scotland), although there remain differences between institutions in the relationship between the governing body, the officers and the senior academic body. As Moodie and Eustace (1974) show, since 1880 governing bodies increasingly took into their ranks members of academic staff, either as representatives of the increasingly powerful Senates or Faculties, and since the 1970s students, with the overall independent majority in some cases down to one or two.

The constituencies from which independent members are drawn vary widely and depend to some extent on the way in which the institution was founded. There are usually local authority nominees and other *ex officio* members such as the nominee of the graduates' association, of a body associated with the foundation of the university (e.g. Merchant Venturers at Bristol) or of another university or college which sponsored the university in earlier days. Otherwise they are people appointed by the University Court (where there is one) or coopted by the governing body from industrial, commercial or professional backgrounds, since they are most likely to bring the required expertise. In some cases some qualification is stipulated,[4] but usually the constituency is left open.

The position in those universities created from 1992 onwards is different. In an attempt to ensure public accountability by preventing these institutions, most of which are former local authority colleges, being dominated by radicals, the independent majority in governing bodies was strengthened in the Education Acts 1988–1992 and in the instruments of government which correspond to the Royal Charters of the older universities. In those institutions with an instrument of government made under this legislation the extraordinary situation has arisen in which there is no legal requirement for any staff or student governors. In Scotland by contrast the Orders of Council made under the Further and Higher Education (Scotland) Act prohibit the governing body from *completely* eliminating either staff or student membership, although it may be reduced to a small minority.

The English legislation[5] prescribes that up to 13 independent members of the governing body shall be chosen from those with experience of, and who have shown capacity in, industrial, commercial or employment matters or the practice of any profession. They may neither be members of staff nor students of the institution nor, to further safeguard against domination by the left, can they be an elected member of a local authority. In addition there is to be at least one and not more than nine coopted members nominated by those members of the governing body who are not themselves coopted members, and which may include members of staff. At least one must have experience in the provision of education; this category also allows for the appointment of elected members of local authorities. Although there is power to appoint or coopt within these maximum and minimum figures, at least half of all members of the board must be independent members.

Independent members tend to be drawn from a restricted section of the population. Although in the survey conducted by Bargh, Scott and Smith (1995), almost 20% of members of governing bodies declined to answer the question 'How do you vote?', not surprisingly of those that did the largest proportion of independent members voted Conservative whereas academic members, particularly those belonging to the 'new' universities tended to vote

Labour or Liberal Democrat. The polarisation in the 'new' universities is particularly significant, with 61% of independent members of governing bodies voting Conservative and 65% of their academic members voting Labour: so it is clear that the legislation had the desired effect. Most governing body members are white (98.2%), male (82.3%), aged 46–65 (70%), educated to at least first degree level and from professional backgrounds (40%) or industry (35%). More than half serve on other public bodies, with the older universities biased towards local authorities, the newer ones towards NHS Trusts and enterprise bodies. Older universities have the highest proportion of retired independent members; overall 55% of independent members are in full-time employment. Ten years ago, the Jarratt Report advocated the appointment of active industrial and business people, particularly outstanding younger executives. Desirable though this might be, it is difficult to reconcile it with the increased demands being placed on independent members, especially as they are unpaid.

Locating the governing body within established models for higher education institutions.

The role of the governing body can be analysed within the established theoretical models of the higher education institution. Davies and Morgan (1983) and Miller (1995) discuss four main organisational models, although these can be grouped in different ways and various composites can be created, as for example, the system perspective suggested by Becher and Kogan (1992). Two can be disposed of quickly:

> The Bureaucratic Model – at one extreme – strict administrative procedures, established by the State or local government, are in place governing everything the university does: innovation is difficult and the role of the chief executive is to make sure the rules are observed. Input from the university community is advisory and there is either no role or only a limited role for independent advisers. Some continental European institutions could be described in these terms: it bears some relation to the way pre-1988 local authority colleges of further and higher education operated but does not apply in the UK today.

> The Ambiguity Model – at the other extreme-either described as 'organized anarchy' as by Cohen and March (1974) or 'garbage can' attributed to Enderud (1977) and further discussed by Walford (1987) where there is an unstructured consideration of issues in what is a loosely structured institution. Elements of informal processes may fit into this model and it might be argued that lack of structure in some of the older universities precipitated some of the crises of earlier days. But the various external controls and reporting requirements, need for strategic plans, estate strategies and the like have probably laid to rest the various forms of the ambiguity model, at least on the institutional scale.

The other two require further consideration. The first is:

> The Collegial Model – the university is considered to be a self-governing body, traditionally dominated by professors, in which as Tavernier (1994) describes it, major decisions are reached 'through all kinds of councils and deliberations' and the role of the chief executive is consensus building. Bargh, Scott and Smith (1995)

describe the mid-twentieth century governing bodies and especially their independent members as being 'on the margins of university government, their effective roles confined to acting as long-stop trustees of their universities, providing a powerful group of 'friends' and offering assistance on restricted topics . . .' such as maintenance of the estate. Ashby and Anderson (1966) clearly took the view, as Hayward (1986) in his analysis of the development of collegial governance between 1880 and 1985 explains, that the independent influence should, like Victorian children, be seen but not heard – or, if heard at all, should be inseparable from the academic.

Changes in public funding and demands for effectiveness, efficiency and economy in the use of funds brought central planning and monitoring firmly onto the agenda in the 1980s. The way in which the universities coped, or failed to cope, with the major retrenchment demanded in the public expenditure cuts of 1981/82 was a catalyst for rapid acceleration of the process by which collegial forms of governance were eroded in most institutions by the managerial and hierarchical forms, and the expertise of members of governing bodies in financial management became more in demand. The recent survey of members of governing bodies by Bargh, Scott and Smith (1995) suggests that the majority of independent members think universities should be run as corporate businesses, with this view held particularly strongly in the new universities.

Can the collegial model now be disregarded? The Jarratt Report[8] recommended that governing bodies 'reassert' themselves over Senates and their equivalent, the clear message being that collegiality was unable to cope with the situation following the end of the quinquennial funding system. As central monitoring of university activities became more explicit following the demise of the academic-dominated University Grants Committee, so the autonomy of Senates was further eroded to the point that academic initiatives could only be taken with some reasonable prospect of adequate funding if they were in conformity with the strategic vision of the non-academic-dominated Funding Councils, which the governing bodies were expected to follow.

From a European perspective Gieseke (1991) holds that '. . . the classical model of self-government as a part-time activity of professors and bodies of professors is no longer sufficient. Many institutions have become big businesses which require an effective management primarily dedicated to this task, both at the level of the institutions and at that of the subject areas.' This is actually a different point. There can be no question that universities are big businesses; while only about 40% of Scottish universities' income is derived from the Funding Council, this alone amounts to over £400m in 1995/96, so that total spending is about £1bn. The concept that they market and provide educational services for reward is enhanced by the image of the student as a customer. Farrington (1992, 1994a, 1994b) analyses the university-student relationship in this way and a number of recent court cases have reinforced this view, for example *Joobeen v University of Stirling* 1995 SLT 120 (Note); *Moran v University College Salford* (1993) Times 23 November.

Effective management in this situation is not necessarily synonymous with the presence of an independent-dominated governing body. As Toyne (1991) argues, an accountable business:

'involves essentially managerial responsibility and accountability of the person labelled, legally, chief executive. This leads to a rise in the central importance of administrative support and administrators in turn become more significant not subservient. Customer-based, accountable businesses is what we are asked to be.'

However, despite the clear message in Halsey's (1992) title *The Decline of Donnish Dominion* those being 'governed' have not yet lost the pass. Bargh, Scott and Smith (1995) report that a return to the collegial form of governance is supported by some 37% of internal members of governing bodies. There is more support for the idea of 'creative' management, the management of networks of creative professionals. How to take account of these views, while at the same time preserving as much as possible of the improvements in efficiency and effectiveness which modern management techniques have brought to universities, is the burning question.

One further theoretical model needs to be considered:

> *The Political Model* – decisions are reached by a process of permanent negotiation between pressure groups with different interests leading to inevitable conflict in times of scarce resources. As things have developed, of all the acknowledged theories we would be hard pressed to argue against the analysis by Baldridge (1971) and Baldridge, Curtis, Ecker and Riley (1978) although the variant suggested by Tavernier (1994) – a 'competitive' model – perhaps approximates most to the current position. In most universities academic managers are expected to run departments under complex resource allocation models, advising and supporting a strong central management in the attainment of objectives set from the centre. The sometimes unpalatable fact is that 'the centre' has less room for manoeuvre. Government policies are put into effect by the Funding Councils, with an increasing tendency to top-slice formula-driven resource allocation models in order to promote inter-institutional competition for funding by means of initiatives of various kinds (technology in teaching, special needs provision, management and administrative computing, library enhancement, extension of the academic year, etc.). Miller (1995) describes the way in which one university adopted a Trading Company Model, in which all departments, including administrative departments, were established as cost centres. It can be argued that widespread devolution of financial decision-making in this way may undermine the power of university constitutional bodies to shape the corporate strategy and to ensure adherence to institutional standards unless the governing body is in a position through monitoring to see that its strategy is put into effect.

Expectations of the governing body

Some variant of the political model, then, is what best describes the current position – an internally competitive model in which the role of the governing body is to set the scene in an informed way and allow the professionals, of which the most important is the Vice-Chancellor or Principal, to manage, deploying such negotiating and consensus-building skills as they can. The tables below set out the expectations of governing bodies from four perspectives: the first three are those of Sizer and Mackie (1994), in their roles as Chief

Executive and Secretary respectively of a Funding Council, of the Committee of University Chairmen (1995) and of the members surveyed by Bargh, Scott and Smith (1995). The fourth is derived by removing the explicitly party political elements from Stewart's (1990) analysis of the expectations of local authorities: comparison of the way chartered universities developed alongside chartered local authorities helps us to understand the history and development of governance and managerial processes before the reforms in both sectors.

1. The Funding Council
[Independent members]:
1. Will act as custodians of the public interest and be responsible for defining strategic objectives to underpin the continuity of existence of the institution to safeguard the pursuit of knowledge and the provision of education.
2. Will act as members of the 'supervisory board' ensuring that the Vice-Chancellor/Principal (Chief Executive) and senior management colleagues act consistently with that strategy and pursue effectively short-term tactics to achieve the institution's goal and mission. and . . .
3. Individual members may advise and assist the institution's management in meeting those managerial responsibilities.

2. Committee of University Chairmen
[The principal roles of members of governing bodies are]:
1. To ensure the proper conduct of public business: observing the highest standards of corporate governance, demonstrating integrity and objectivity and wherever possible following a policy of openness and transparency in the dissemination of decisions.
2. In strategic planning: enabling the institution to achieve and develop its primary objectives of teaching and research: this includes considering and approving the institution's strategic plan.
3. In finance: approving operating plans and budgets reflecting the strategic plan; ensuring solvency of the institution and safeguarding its assets; ensuring that funds provided by the Funding Council are used in accordance with the terms and conditions attached by the Council in pursuance of their powers under the Further and Higher Education Acts; receiving and approving the annual accounts; ensuring the existence and integrity of financial control systems.
4. In estates: considering, approving and keeping under review the Estate Strategy required by the Funding Council: this strategy identifies the property and space requirements needed to fulfil the objectives of the strategic plan and also allows for a planned programme of maintenance.

3. Survey of Members
[Members see their role mainly as]:
1. Setting overall strategy (56.2% of respondents seeing this role as becoming of greater importance in the future).

2.   Audit, ie ensuring that the policies of the governing body are carried out in an efficient way.

3.   Supervising the chief executive and other senior managers.

4.   Giving technical advice.

5.   Ensuring that local community/business voices are heard.

4.   Local authority analogy

[The functions of members of the governing body are]:

1.   Acting corporately to be responsible for setting directions, policy-making and resource allocation. Although legally responsible for policy implementation and operational management, they cannot carry this out directly but must ensure that there is an adequate framework for the effective management of the institution in accordance with the governing body's policies. They require procedures and settings that assist that task and can draw upon officer advice, information and guidance.

2.   Acting corporately to be responsible for review and control to ensure that their policy is implemented and the need for policy change high-lighted and to ensure the adequacy of arrangements for the management of the institution, including arrangement for operational control.

but . . .

3.   Individual members' direct involvement in operational management will normally prevent rather than assist effective management.

From all these perspectives the effective institution is one in which the responsibility of the governing body for setting directions, supervising policy implementation and management are clear but in which the need for direct intervention by members, particularly independent members, is limited because adequate management processes have been set up to achieve the governing body's objectives. As Sizer and Mackie (1994) say, these are 'exacting expectations' for unpaid people giving up valuable time, particularly when the Financial Memorandum between the Funding Council and the university imposes certain specific duties on the governing body. It is clear that the governing body is itself responsible for ensuring that funds from the Council are used only in accordance with the terms of the legislation, the Memorandum and any conditions which the Council is lawfully able to prescribe.

There are problems with some of the statements in the tables, particularly the first, which gives members of governing bodies a heavy responsibility as 'custodians of the public interest', not how most would see their role. In the survey by Bargh, Scott and Smith (1995), members were not asked this question explictly, but were asked about the importance of representing the community. This was ranked below roles of strategic planning, audit, supervising the chief executive and management and supporting the university, but above direct managerial input, appeals and negotiating. Originally, in England, the 'custodian of the public interest' was the University Court, a body with much wider membership than the governing body with, as Morrell (1986) says 'vague or slight powers' and seen as a means by which the university could account to its wider public. The statement by Hayward (1986) that the governing body is the 'executive committee of the Court' is questionable but the boundaries do need to be defined, since in some university charters the Court is called the 'Supreme Governing Body . . . with absolute power'. Farrington (1994) suggests that the Court has residual power where the governing body is hopelessly deadlocked or legally incapable of deciding some issue, on the analogy with a company general meeting. The principal difficulty is of course that, as at general meetings, attendance at the Court is notoriously light and the expense of having a Court is difficult to justify. In practice, the public interest in the work of universities can be met by a requirement for an annual report to the Funding Council.

There is also the Visitor, whose jurisdiction is a medieval relic, but who may make final and binding determinations on virtually anything and retains the rarely (if ever) used power to 'direct an inspection.'[7] The Visitorial jurisdiction is useful in providing a cheap source of high quality arbiters in personal grievances but that is about the limit of its usefulness today and its remaining functions should be abolished.

The process of 'supervising' the chief executive is also problematic, since the Financial Memorandum requires the governing body to appoint an individual (normally the chief executive) as the accounting officer. This officer can, if he/she feels it necessary to do so, go over the head of the governing body, his/her employer, to the Funding Council where that body is, in his/her opinion, taking action incompatible with the terms of the Memorandum. It is the accounting officer who would have to explain the actions of the university to the National Audit Office and, in the last resort, to the Public Accounts Committee. The accounting officer is then placed in a similar position to the permanent head of a government department or executive agency, with the governing body replaced by ministers but the analogy breaks down when the officer is him/herself an executive governor. In many of the older universities the Vice-Chancellor's powers are theoretically extremely limited, although in the newer constitutions it is clear that the governing body delegates day to day management control to its chief executive. These complications require to be resolved in any new structure.

Governors and directors

There has been a tendency to draw analogies between independent governors and non-executive directors – for example Sizer and Mackie (1994) take the view that 'the role of independent governors may be equated with that of paid non-executive directors'. The implied analogy between a board of directors and a governing body is in my view wide of the mark for the following reasons:.

Composition of boards

Company boards consist of executive directors who are senior managers and generally a smaller number of non-executive directors, all having the same duties and responsibilities under common law and statute. In university governing bodies the independent members are in the majority, in some cases a large majority. The academics and students who make up the minority (in some cases a small minority) cannot be equated with executive directors, the only exceptions being the Vice-Chancellor or Principal (chief executive) with perhaps one or more Pro-Vice-Chancellors or Deputy/Vice-Principals. Except where individual members of the governing body have particular powers or duties derived either from the instrument of government (perhaps as a Pro-Chancellor, a Treasurer or other named officer) or from the operation of common law (as the chair of a meeting), or where they under some partial disadvantage (as are students in respect of personal [reserved] business) they are all legally equal, independent, academic and student members alike. As a general principle they act together either *as* the corporation which conducts the university (in the case of the new universities and the non-chartered Scottish universities) or *as that organ of* the corporation charged with executive authority over resources (as in the chartered bodies where the university itself is the corporation).

Although generally speaking all members have an equal say and equal vote, it is common to find in the standing orders of the older universities a requirement for minimum quora of both independent and academic members; this is not normally the case in the newer institutions.

Personal accountability

The lack of personal accountability also distinguishes members of university governing bodies from directors of companies.[8] Well-known realist theories of corporate personality emphasise the possession by a corporation of a metaphysical personality independent of its members and this is as true in commercial companies as it is in charitable corporations with perpetual succession. However, if we analyse group responsibility in the way Dworkin (1986) has done, we may put forward the proposition that only those entitled to share in the profits of a corporation (such as the directors or, in Dworkin's example the accounts of shareholders) must share in its responsibilities. That is a principle which cannot be applied to university governors: there are no profits in which to share and they have no (or certainly should not have any) financial interest in the corporation, other than as employees (staff) or customers (students). Although the issue has not explicitly been tested in the courts in modern times, it appears that they have no individual liability.[9] The only action, other than an ordinary action for breach of contract, tort, etc which may be taken against a chartered university council which is alleged to have exceeded its powers is for a member of the corporation, or possibly the Attorney-General, to apply to the Crown for revocation of the charter.[10] Action against statutory corporations or limited companies follow the normal processes of law in relation to acts alleged to be *ultra vires*, but in any of these cases, no action can normally be taken against individuals.

Directors, who may be employees of the corporation, are also its agents and have a fiduciary relationship to the corporation as principal, with duties similar to those of a trustee. As persons in receipt of financial reward they have legal duties to act in the interests of the corporation and not to allow conflicts of interest to arise: not to make a 'secret profit' or otherwise act improperly. Directors must act within their powers with such care as can reasonably be expected of people in their position having regard to their own experience and skills. Although the legal definition of a director is a circular one: '. . . a person occupying the position of a director by whatever name called'[11] the relationship of a director to the corporation and his or her powers emanate from the Articles of Association and any service contract he or she may have. The role of governor is however not taken on for personal financial gain, indeed it is common to see independent members elevated to academic degrees *honoris causa* as the only tangible way of recognising their contribution.[12] Bargh, Scott and Smith (1995) demonstrate that independent members largely see the job in personal terms: they take it on because they see themselves as having appropriate skills and experience. Academic members see it more in collective terms, with their role as delegates or representatives, although in fact they are not legally in that position but share the same responsibilities as the independent members.

On the other hand, there are some aspects of the work of non-executive directors and independent members of governing bodies which are similar and the analogy may assist us in formulating a new model:

Duties of non-executive directors

The main duties of a non-executive director are to contribute an independent view, help the board to provide the company with effective leadership, ensure the continuing effectiveness of the executive directors and management, and ensure high standards of financial probity.[13] These duties bear a close relationship to those identified for independent members by Sizer and Mackie and by the Committee of University Chairmen. More recently there has been a call for the adoption of formal processes for the appointment of non-executive directors, who should also have a specific term of appointment and this is being followed through in universities: the circumstances in which directors and independent members can be removed are also broadly similar.[14] Non-executive directors typically give 15–20 days per annum to the company bringing outside knowledge, expertise and experience to the board's deliberations. The survey by Bargh, Scott and Smith (1995) shows that outside formal meetings of the governing body (say six days per annum), the majority of independent members spend one or two days per month on university business, although a quarter of respondents spent no time on business outside formal meetings. Personal experience suggests that those members who are appointed *ex officio*, for example the chairman of the local authority, spend much less time than those appointed with professional backgrounds, where the total attendance can easily reach 30 days per annum, considerably more than is expected of many non-executive directors.

Audit and remuneration committees

Non-executive directors normally serve on audit and remuneration committees, and this practice is increasingly followed in universities. Indeed an Audit

Committee must be established under the Financial Memorandum and it has to be independent of the financial management of the institution with direct access to the Funding Council if necessary. A remuneration committee is now almost *de rigeur* following the Public Accounts Committee report on severance payments[15] and advice given by the Committee of University Chairmen, followed up by the Nolan Committee on Standards in Public Life. Institutions will in future be required to disclose the salaries of their chief executives and other senior staff, in a format similar to that used in company accounts. Following the PAC report, media interest has disclosed considerable variation in these salary levels.

Right to obtain information

Non-executive directors are expected to call for information to satisfy themselves as to the propriety of a course of action and that it is in the best interests of the company. They cannot rely on the fact that action is recommended by the executive members. Pahl and Winkler (1974) argue that board actions may best be interpreted as ratification of decisions made earlier and elsewhere, sometimes by more junior people and about which the board had no practical alternative: as Hayward (1986) points out, that is equally true of university governing bodies. In that sense, it is extremely difficult for non-executive directors or independent members to ensure that the plans of the organisation are prudent enough to cope with the volatility of the environment in which they operate, although the Funding Councils themselves take care to check that the financial forecasts are consistent with such volatility as is inevitable in a constantly changing system.

It is difficult to be clear about the extent to which independent members of governing bodies can have a direct and truly 'independent' influence on the institution's planning, on its performance against plans and how realistic the planning is in the context of the funding environment. The question must be how 'involved' members feel and whether the quality of information made available to them is adequate to enable informed judgements to be made. It is worth noting that, by analogy with the position of members of local authorities, members of governing bodies, at any rate those of institutions with a charter, have no common law right to see documents just out of curiosity, but only where there is a reasonable need to do so (*R v Southwold Corporation, ex p Wrightson* (1907) 5 LGR 888; *R v Barnes Borough Council, ex p Conlan* [1938] 3 All ER 226; *R v Lancashire County Council Police Authority, ex p Hook* [1980] QB 603) and that is a potential difficulty. In some sensitive areas, a 'need to know' principle may be invoked. (*R v Birmingham City Council, ex p O* [1983] 1 AC 578.)

Funding Councils recognise that members of governing bodies must have readily comprehensible information about the way they discharge their responsibilities. An example given by Sizer and Mackie (1994) is the much greater transparency in the method of funding of teaching than existed under former arrangements. By making this information available in the way they do, the Councils hope that it is more possible for independent governors to make decisions on the basis of informed personal judgment than through reliance on executive recommendations. The requirement that strategic plans and financial forecasts must be explicitly approved by the governing body reinforces the responsibility of that body. In the university context, this depends on members knowing what information to call for and then being reasonably satisfied that what is provided is of sufficient quality to enable them to make informed judgments.

In the survey by Bargh, Scott and Smith (1995), 74% of external members were satisfied with the relevance of the information received, but only 53% of internal members: this can presumably be attributed to the internal members' greater knowledge of the 'system.' Standing Orders provide mechanisms by which members may ensure that due notice is given of business to be transacted and other procedures followed, and the post-1992 universities have spelt out the quorum rules in their Articles of Association. The post-1992 institutions have also spelt out clearly what matters may not be delegated to committees or officers, whereas in older institutions virtually anything may be delegated if the governing body so resolves. The governing body is also entitled to rely on its secretary to ensure that it is acting within its legal powers.[16] It is, of course, necessary that this officer has the required knowledge and expertise and this is one area in which the Funding Councils have a legitimate right to be satisfied.

A possible model for the future

I start from the proposition that the *status quo* cannot be defended. Even before 1992 there was considerable variation; now there can be no doubt that there is no single agreed system of governance in universities which are all trying to do the same job. The old collegial model has fallen away, leaving academics unsure of their role in managing the institution; and in the formal setting there are a number of possible areas of conflict between institutional leaders, professional managers and their governing bodies in what is a highly political and competitive environment. Lurking behind the scenes in many of the older universities is the unresolved positions of the Court and the Visitor and the personal responsibility of all members of governing bodies, including the executive members, has to be clearly spelt out.

Everything depends, however, on the way institutions are funded because the role of governing bodies hinges on their responsibilities. It is not the purpose of this paper to propound the economic arguments for 'opting-out' or any other form of relaxing state control – even a cursory look at the figures shows how difficult a task it would be to raise the sums now managed by the Funding Councils[17] – but such a course would certainly make it much easier to define a role for governing bodies. If tuition fees were paid by the customers, with government scholarships available to the best qualified, and, after the one-off transfer of all publicly-funded assets to the independent corporations, direct government funding ceased, competitive markets would exist for all purposes, including research, funding for which is an important component of the Funding Council allocation formulae.

In this market place universities would be run as private charitable corporations or trusts. The need for highly qualified management expertise would increase, as it has in the National Health Service and Executive Agencies. Although subject to accreditation, withdrawal of which would simply result in customers putting their business elsewhere, and obtaining relevant quality kitemarks, universities would be wholly responsible for their survival and lose the bureaucracy associated with state control. Government would be in the hands of boards of management or trustees made up largely of universities' own executives and elected representatives of the staff and students, with paid non-executive directors brought in to perform the duties they fulfil elsewhere. The respective roles of managers and governing bodies could be clearly delineated, and Courts replaced by consultative meetings.

It is not necessary to go this far to achieve reform of governance, retaining what is best from the traditional universities and blending it with good practice from the new institutions and the corporate sector. The Funding Councils, quite properly, insist on high standards of financial management and universities will always wish to call upon experienced people from relevant backgrounds to help them to manage effectively. But without reducing their accountability to the public they do not need to have their calendars cluttered with useless formality. The model I wish to suggest is:

1.   Abolition of the Court (or its equivalent) and those powers of the Visitor which do not relate to personal grievances and disputes.

2.   Executive power in all universities placed exclusively in the governing body with full power to delegate to committees or officers on any matter except approval of the institution's budget, accounts, and the appointment/dismissal of senior officers and auditors.

3.   The governing body to be a board with executive and non-executive members, with executive members being in the voting majority, perhaps along these lines:

     A non-executive Chairman
     The Chief Executive (Vice-Chancellor/Principal)
     One or more Deputy Chief Executives (including a General Manager)
     Up to 12 Executive Directors (Academic) (Deans, etc.)
     3 Executive Directors (Non-Academic)
     5 Non-Executive Directors (paid)
     with a legally-qualified non-voting Secretary

This results in a governing body of about 25 members at most, with a proportionately smaller body for smaller institutions. Although the maximum size is relatively large compared with many company boards, it is essential in an academic institution that major stakeholders such as Deans of Faculties feel ownership of decisions. Even the private University of Buckingham has a governing body of 38, including up to 16 coopted members.[18]

The proposed structure places the power in the internal affairs of the institution back in the hands of its own staff, since the academic executive directors who manage the 'creative networks' represent the collegium. The significant change from the present arrangements is that they, together with the chief executive and at least one academic deputy chief executive, control the balance of power, although the constitution should prescribe that no decision on non-academic issues should validly be taken without participation by both academic and independent members. The proposed arrangement enables the political or competitive model of governance to operate within a system which also places the chief executive in a position of authority, since it would be to him/her that the majority of day-to-day power was devolved and it would be the chief executive who answered, as now, to the Funding Council as accounting officer. This, in itself, is sufficient to answer concerns that academics would be unable to govern the newest universities, as they already successfully govern the oldest.

The model preserves the role of the independent member as an expert adviser but enhances this by payment, so hopefully increasing the range of people able to make an active contribution while in employment elsewhere. Non-executive members would continue to make up the audit and remuneration committees but would not be expected to spend more than 15–20 days per annum on university business.

It would be a straightforward exercise to amend the legislation, charters and other instruments of government; the formal powers of governing bodies and the role and responsibilities of Senates, Academic Boards, etc. need be unaffected. A constitution would be drawn up in which it would be clear that members bear no personal liability for corporate decisions taken *intra vires*; alternatively liability insurance would be purchased on their behalf. It would be the professional duty of the Secretary to advise the governing body on such matters.

I believe this model is also readily adaptable to the hypothetical scenario in which universities become more like private corporations or trusts. Whether or not universities continue to be funded as they are at present, the model establishes clear lines of responsibility, a real role for the academic staff and offers the opportunity for recruitment of well-qualified, younger people to occupy the position of non-executive governor.

Notes

1. Strictly, in those new universities 'conducted' by higher education corporations, the members of the governing body are the members of the corporation but the practical effect is the same.
2. The term 'independent' is synonymous with 'lay' for the purposes of this paper, although in the traditional universities lay membership includes local authority members *ex officio*.
3. In the older universities the majority of independent members may be only one or two.
4. For example in one English university, of the ten coopted members it is

desirable that 'at least one shall be a Fellow of the Royal Society and at least five shall hold or have held positions of distinction in industrial or commercial undertakings or bodies engaged in research'.

5. Schedule 7A Education Reform Act 1988.
6. Committee of Vice-Chancellors and Principals *Report of the Steering Committee for Efficiency Studies (The Jarratt Report)* London CVCP 1985.
7. This is one way in which the government could have imposed quality assurance and assessment systems on English chartered universities without legislation.
8. In universities conducted by companies limited by guarantee, the governing body also acts as the board of directors of the company.
9. The commonly accepted rule so far as non-chartered bodies are concerned is that in *R v Watson* (1788) 2 Term Rep 199; ie that individual members are not liable for corporate acts except that if the act concerned is *ultra vires* and proves to be tortious or delictual the members who authorised the act might themselves be sued, particularly if the act complained of was wilful and malicious.
10. As this legal point is not crystal clear, the Funding Councils advise institutions to take out insurance against the costs of any claims of negligence which may be made against members of the governing body in carrying out their duties.
11. Section 741 Companies Act 1985.
12. The Nolan Committee on Standards in Public Life has turned its attention to education, in particular looking at the mechanisms for appointing officers and staff of institutions and any safeguards in place against potential conflicts of interest.
13. See, for example, the 1972 BIM Survey quoted in the *Report of the Committee of Inquiry into Industrial Democracy (The Bullock Report)*, 1977 Cmnd 6706.
14. The articles of most companies provide for vacation of office by a director either on reaching a specified age limit, on becoming of unsound mind, on being absent from meetings for a period without good cause, on bankruptcy or making arrangements with creditors, on conviction of certain offences relating to companies, fraud, breach of duty etc. and a director can in certain circumstances be disqualified for a period of years. The circumstances in which members of governing bodies may be removed by the body vary just as the constitutions vary: in the chartered universities removal is sanctioned by specified majority vote for 'good cause' (generally interpreted as criminal conviction for a serious crime, serious misconduct, inability to discharge functions through physical or mental incapacity): examples from the 'new' sector include sequestration of estate, bankruptcy, entering into arrangements with creditors, physical or mental illness (Glasgow Caledonian University) and where 'continuation would bring discredit on the name of the University or in such other circumstances as the Court may determine and record in a standing order.' (University of Paisley).

15. Committee of Public Accounts, 28th Report, 14 June 1995.
16. The legal powers of a chartered corporation are extremely wide: the only practical controls are those of charitable status and requirements to abide by terms and conditions laid down by those who provide funding: the Funding Councils, research sponsors and others.
17. Although these figures must be regarded as very approximate, given the definitions used by SHEFC, withdrawal of £400m from the 13 universities spread over 103,000 students 'eligible for funding' represents a public subsidy of almost £4000 per student. In addition, 26% of income came from academic fees: although this figure includes full cost fees paid from private sources, it is largely public funding through education authorities and government departments, representing a further public subsidy of perhaps £2500 per head. Research grants and services rendered, which would also operate on a competitive market, account at present for a further 23% of income, with only 2% from donations and endowments, the balance being a miscellany of trading activities and other minor items.
18. Appendix to *Quality Audit Report, University of Buckingham*, HEQC 1993.

References

Ashby, E. and Anderson, A., 1966. *Universities: British, Indian, African. A Study in the Ecology of Higher Education.* London: Weidenfield & Nicholson.

Baldridge, J., 1971. *Power and Conflict in the University.* New York: John Wiley.

Baldridge, J., Curtis, D., Ecker, G. and Riley, G., 1978. *Policy Making and Effective Leadership.* San Francisco: Jossey-Bass.

Bargh, C., Scott, P. and Smith, D., 1995. *Changing Patterns of Governance in Higher Education.* Leeds: Centre for Policy Studies in Education.

Becher, T. and Kogan, M., 1992. *Process and Structure in Higher Education.* London: Routledge.

Boyer, E.L., Altbach, P.G. and Whitelaw, M.J., 1994. *The Academic Profession: an International Perspective – a special report.* New York: Carnegie Foundation for the Advancement of Teaching.

Cohen, M. and March, J., 1974. *Leadership and Ambiguity.* New York: McGraw Hill.

Committee of University Chairmen, 1995. *Guide for Members of Governing Bodies of Universities and Colleges in England and Wales.*

Davies, J.L. and Morgan, A.W., 1983. Management of Higher Education Institutions in a Period of Contraction and Uncertainty. In Boyd-Barrett,O., Bush,T., Goodey, J., McNay I. and Preedy, M., (eds), *Approaches to Post-School Management.* London: Harper & Row.

Dworkin, R., 1986. *Law's Empire.* London: Fontana.

Ellis, E. L., 1972. *The University College of Wales at Aberystwyth.* Cardiff: University of Wales.

Enderud, H., 1977. *Four Faces of Leadership in an Academic Organisation.* Copenhagen: Nyt Nordisk, Forlag Arnold Busck.

Farrington, D.J., 1992. The University-Student Contract. *Journal of Educational Administration and History* **24(2)** 197.

Farrington, D.J., 1994a. *The Law of Higher Education.* London: Butterworths.

Farrington, D.J., 1994b. Students and The Law. In Haselgrove, S., (ed), *The Student*

Experience. Buckingham: Society for Research into Higher Education & Open University Press.

Fielden, J. and Lockwood, G., 1973. *Planning and Management in Universities: A Study of British Universities.* London: Chatto and Windus.

Giesecke, L., 1991. The Humboldt Principles of the University and their significance for contemporary mass higher education. *Paper for the Standing Conference on University Problems (CC-PU) Council of Europe, Strasbourg 19–21 March.*

Halsey, A.H., 1992. *The Decline of Donnish Dominion.* Oxford: Clarendon Press.

Handy, C.B., 1977. The Organisations of Consent. In Warren Piper, D. and Glatter, R., (eds), *The Changing University.* Slough: NFER.

Hayward, J.C.F., 1986. University Councils in Times of Change. In Bosworth, S.R., (ed), *Beyond The Limelight: Essays on the occasion of the Silver Jubilee of the Conference of University Administrators.* Reading: Conference of University Administrators.

Hearnshaw, F.J.C., 1929. *The Centenary History of King's College.* London: Harrap.

Miller, H.D.R., 1995. *The Management of Change in Universities.* London: SRHE and Open University Press.

Moodie, G.C. and Eustace, R., 1974. *Power and Authority in British Universities.* London: Allen & Unwin pp 33–44.

Morrell, D.W.J., 1986. Universities and their Communities. In Bosworth, S.R., (ed), *Beyond The Limelight: Essays on the occasion of the Silver Jubilee of the Conference of University Administrators.* Reading: Conference of University Administrators.

Pahl, R.E. and Winkler, J.J., 1974. The Economic Elite: Theory and Practice. In Stanworth, P. and Giddens, A., (eds), *Elites and Power in British Society.* Cambridge University Press.

Sizer, J. and Mackie, D., 1994. *Greater Accountability: The Price of Autonomy.* Edinburgh: Scottish Higher Education Funding Council.

Stewart, J., 1990. The Role of Councillors in the Management of the Authority. *Local Government Studies* July/August 25.

Tavernier, K., 1994. Managing a University: challenges and opportunities. *Council of Europe seminar, Tashkent.*

Toyne, P., 1991. Appropriate Structures for Higher Education Institutions. *Paper presented to the International Seminar on Management in Universities, British Council, Brighton, July.*

Walford, G., 1987. *Restructuring Universities: Politics and Power in the Management of Change.* Beckenham: Croom Helm.

Welch, R., 1995. Rise of the managerial cadre. *Times Higher Educational Supplement* 16 June.

Whiting, C.E., 1932. *The University of Durham 1832–1932.* London: Sheldon Press.

Gazza and Greenbury: similarities and differences

Stefan Szymanski

> 'One day this country will decide that good businessmen are entitled to be paid at least as much as good footballers. Personally I am all in favour of good footballers being paid quite a lot, but a guy who runs his business quite success-fully, and is as good at running a business as a footballer is at scoring goals deserves to be paid.'
> Kenneth Clarke, Chancellor of the Exchequer, reported in the Financial Times, 16th March 1995

> 'Chief executives point out with some bitterness that the British public is more accepting of high rewards for pop stars and sportsmen than for businessmen.'
> Editorial, Financial Times, 28th January 1995

> 'As a society we have adopted an odd set of priorities over remuneration. We put a high price on escapism (pop stars, footballers, film stars, lottery winners). Entrepreneurs and well-heeled professionals go largely beyond rebuke. But we quibble about the often much smaller sums that go to bosses of the major companies which underpin our economy.'
> Iain Vallance, Chairman of British Telecom, Financial Times, 25th January 1995

Introduction

Public opinion seems deeply hostile to the levels of directors' pay in public corporations. Some argue that this hostility is merely a reflection of jealousy; others that it reflects ignorance of workings of industry and finance. Among the defences attempted by supporters of current directors' pay levels perhaps the most colourful is the contrast with the pay levels of professional football players. In effect the argument is this: if a centre forward can be paid a fortune for what he does, why not the chief executive of a plc? This paper will explore that question.

The paper describes three notions of fairness, according to which the pay of directors and professional footballers can be compared: procedural fairness, distributive fairness and market efficiency. These are described in the next section. In the following section the history of pay setting, first for directors and second for professional footballers, is analyzed according to each notion of fairness. Finally, the paper considers the implications of the Greenbury Report and its relevance to pay setting for executives.

The main argument presented in this paper is that the pay setting of professional footballers conforms closely to the idealised notion of an efficient market. The pay setting of directors however, falls some way short of this ideal. To the extent that any single football player might be criticised for being over paid, the counter-argument can almost always be raised that the player in question could get more or less exactly the same terms at a rival club. Company directors tend not to be readily transferable, and the notion of a market for directors scarcely exists. This does not of itself mean that directors are over paid. However if the pay setting procedure for directors is also flawed, in the sense of giving the directors themselves a decisive influence over setting their own pay, then the wages paid will inevitably appear unfair.

Fairness and pay

How does hostility to the executive pay levels come about? A plausible answer is that independent observers consider that they are not fair. Fairness in the context of pay has three aspects:

Procedural fairness

If the procedure by which the rate of pay for a job is determined is considered unfair, then usually the outcome of the procedure (the pay settlement) will be considered unfair. Procedure means the process of evaluation, both of the employee's performance, the performance of the business and general market conditions. It also means the process of negotiation by which a decision is reached, the choice of decision makers and the justification for the final decision (including any appeals procedure). A procedure may be unfair regardless of the level of pay itself. This might be because of lack of consultation, failure to give due weight to relevant factors and so on. If the outcome is considered fair, then an unfair process is likely to pass without much comment. But even in cases where, for example, a trade union is made an offer which it is willing to accept, it would be unlikely to do so if it were denied the right to consult with the employer and bargain over the offer. In practice, however, the fairness of wage offers is almost always debatable, and in the absence of an objective measure of a fair outcome, procedural unfairness may weigh very heavily in the opinions of observers.

The just wage and the market

A second notion of unfairness is that the rate of pay does not adequately compensate the contribution of the employee; this is the opposite of the notion of 'a fair day's work for a fair day's pay'. In this sense a pay rate may be deemed unfair because of the level of effort required, the unpleasantness of the job, the level of prior education and training required or the risks involved. This idea has a long history, at least as far back as St Thomas Aquinas who wrote about the just wage. The problem with the idea of a just wage is that reasonable people may differ on what is just, and that therefore the notion provides no practical guide as to how wages should be fixed.

Economists, concerned with the practicalities of wage setting, have, since Adam Smith, argued that an individual's remuneration cannot be considered independently of the market for his services. Thus the appropriate rate of pay for a job is that which is just sufficient to attract enough people into that particular employment to satisfy the demand for the goods or services produced on the job. This means that given the rate of pay, there is no unsatisfied demand for the good or service and no excess supply unsold. This mechanism for setting pay has the advantage of being self regulating in a free market (no one need accept a job paying less than the market rate, and no employer need pay more).

The operation of a market does not mean that all employees will be paid the same. Adam Smith argued that differences in wage rates could be accounted for by one of five possible factors, now known as compensating differentials:

1. The ease or hardship, the cleanliness or dirtiness, the honourableness or dishonourableness of the employment.

2. The easiness and cheapness, or the difficulty and expense of learning the business.

3. The constancy or inconstancy of employment.

4. The small or great trust which must be reposed in the workmen.

5. The probability or improbability of success in employment:
   (Smith (1981: 117–122)).

Thus, unless there is some obstacle to the operation of the market, for an economist it is in principle impossible for a pay rate to be unjust in the sense of not offering a wage which adequately compensates the effort provided. For example, even if it is agreed that nurses have low pay, the argument goes, they are still being paid enough to make it worthwhile for them to come work. If the pay rate is unfair, the unfairness resides elsewhere.

Distributive fairness

Even if the rate of pay for a job reflects the operations of the market it still might be considered unfair in a distributive sense. Distributive fairness is a relative notion. When the data are available, individuals are always drawn to making comparisons between pay rates. Pay rates are often taken as proxies for the relative worth of the individuals in a wider sense and therefore a pay rate may be considered unfair if it does not accurately reflect the perceived relative worth of an individual. Thus, comparing the pay of nurses and policemen, many people argue that the pay of nurses is unfair, because in their view nurses are just as valuable as policemen but receive lower pay.

There is a tension between the kind of fairness implicit in the notions of market efficiency and distributive fairness. For example, it could be said that collecting household rubbish is a job which is not only unpleasant but also indispensable for a modern society and that therefore the pay rate for the job should be among the highest in society. But, because there is a ready supply of people willing to do this job, pay rates are in fact relatively low. Whilst most people can see the logic in the second argument, they are uncomfortable with it.

In the rest of this paper the pay setting of senior company executives and professional footballers will be evaluated according to the three criteria set out here: procedural fairness, market efficiency and distributive fairness.

Procedural fairness

Directors

The origins of the public furore over executive pay lie in two factors, firstly the obligation to publish pay levels, secondly the historical lack of any transparent mechanism for setting pay levels. The first step towards publishing individual pay levels in the UK occurred in the 1967 Companies Act in which public quoted corporations were required to state the aggregate of base pay plus bonuses paid to the highest paid director[1].

It is a frequent complaint of directors that they are obliged to reveal data on their salaries while other highly paid professionals such as lawyers and accountants are not. However, it is worth noting that the trend toward disclosure has accompanied the increasing dominance of insurance companies and pensions funds in the ownership of plcs through the stock market. For example in 1963 over 50% of shares on the London Stock Market were owned by private individuals of whom there was a relatively small number. Insurance companies and pension funds owned only 15% of the market. Consequently few people had any financial interest, as owners, in the behaviour of quoted companies. By 1992 over 50% of shares were owned by pension funds and insurance companies, while 60% of full time employees had a pension scheme. Through such indirect mechanisms a majority of households have come to have a stake in the performance of quoted companies, and also in the pay setting process of directors.

As the 1980s progressed, it became plain for all to see that company directors were enjoying very high and rapidly increasing rates of pay. Naturally enough, commentators began to ask who was sanctioning these increases and what they were supposed to achieve. At the same time, the more general issue of corporate governance, the way in which decision making in large corporations is structured, came into question (see for example Jenkinson and Mayer (1992) for a survey). Issues raised included the rights of shareholders to influence company policies, checks on the discretion of directors, the role of non-executive directors and so on. All these concerns shared a particular root.

By the 1950s and 1960s it had become apparent that large publicly quoted companies dominated the economic life of the country, and that these corporations were run on a day-to-day basis by a small group of men (always men at that time), the board of directors. In principle, shareholders could pass resolutions at Annual General Meetings to direct company policy. In practice ownership was fragmented, with even the largest shareholder typically owning less than 10% of the company, so that a coalition of shareholders sufficient to gain over 50% of the votes needed to be so large as to be unrealistic. Furthermore, the largest shareholders who were now the Institutions (primarily insurance companies and pension funds) made it clear that they had no interest in interfering in the day-to-day running of the company or proposing resolutions at AGMs.

At the beginning of the 1980s it appeared to outsiders that it was perfectly feasible for a company chairman or chief executive to set his own pay rate. Thus, in a typical situation, the board would set up a sub-committee to examine senior pay, the chairman might also chair the committee and then be present in the room, contribute to the debate and then vote, if not on his own salary, then at least on that of other board members and senior executives. For example, in a survey Conyon (1994) found that in 1988 only 53% of quoted companies in the sample had remuneration committees, while even in 1993 41% of chief executive officers sat on the remuneration committee. Since no company was at that time obliged to reveal publicly the process, the extent to which the system was abused cannot be precisely gauged. However, off the record, many salary consultants will admit that abuses were not uncommon in the 'bad old days'. To many observers, this state of affairs was procedurally unfair, since it allowed a few privileged individuals to write themselves blank cheques using someone else's cheque book[2].

Towards the end of the 1980s concern with the process of corporate governance in general and executive pay setting in particular led to a series of initiatives. First, the Cadbury Committee on Corporate Governance made a number of recommendations on the pay setting process. These included the establishment of remuneration committees chaired in all cases by a non-executive (Cadbury (1992)). Second, the Greenbury Report (1995), given enormous status by the backing of the Government, proposed further advances in disclosure, particularly in relation to pension contributions, and proposed a code of practice on executive pay determination.

To what extent have these Committees and Reports dealt with the problem originally identified, that board directors were essentially in a position to set their own pay? Would a reasonable observer still consider pay setting procedurally unfair? While no legal restraint exists to prevent the continuation of old practices, many of the recommendations have been adopted by influential bodies such as the London Stock Exchange and the Association of British Insurers (ABI) and so failure to comply with guidelines can be sanctioned through serious penalties such as suspension of stock exchange listing. Formally speaking therefore, the answer must be that board members should never find themselves in the position of voting, directly or indirectly on their own pay increases. On the other hand, board directors, particularly chairmen and chief executives, retain considerable powers to influence the process indirectly. Their power to appoint sympathetic non-executive directors remains and while they may not directly appoint external consultants there is inevitably scope for informal pressure, in the same way that accounting companies which act as auditors face implicit conflicts of interest when they carry out consultancy as well as auditing functions.

The fundamental problem which remains, even when codes of best practice are implemented, is that board members are extremely powerful figures in their own right, and, like politicians, are in a position to influence events. It is very unlikely that such people will ever be free from the accusation that they are manipulating events in order to line their own pockets, whether they are doing so or not.

Footballers

In terms of the pay setting process the experience of professional footballers is precisely the reverse of senior executives. That is to say they have progressed from a position where they had virtually no say in the setting of their own pay, to a position where they now possess considerable bargaining power. At the beginning of the 1960s they had so little influence over the wage and employment situation they were considered little better than slaves. By the 1990s there were many in the football industry, notably managers and club chairmen, who argued that players had too much say in determining their own rewards.

This reversal of fortunes has been mirrored by sports leagues throughout the world, most notably in the Baseball and American Football Leagues[3]. Uniquely among private sector employers, the owners of sports teams in professional leagues maintained a system by which individual players were prevented from selling their services freely in the market. Up until 1961 the British system (practised in both the English and Scottish Leagues) had two elements. Firstly there was a maximum wage fixed by the clubs, which in 1961 was £20 per week during the season and £17 per week in the summer (Walvin (1994)). This was a considerable premium to the industrial wage levels which most players would have earned had they not been blessed with talent. Given that most players felt they were being paid to do what they loved best, there was remarkably little agitation against the maximum. The second restriction made the salary cap stick, and that was the 'retain and transfer' system which endowed a player's club with his registration: his license to play professional football. Without this, a player could not play in the Football League. Therefore players could only move to other clubs with the permission of their own club, and no bidding war could break out between clubs to attract players. When a player was transferred, the fee was paid to the club and the player had no share in the proceeds. Clubs competed to attract playing talent either by acquiring players (somewhat speculatively) at the beginning of their career or by bribery and corruption.

This palpable procedural unfairness was dismantled in the early 1960s. Firstly the Professional Footballers Association (the PFA, the players union) under Jimmy Hill managed to get the maximum wage abolished in 1961.

Secondly, in 1963 the High Court ruled in a test case that clubs could not prevent players moving to other clubs when out of contract and asserted the basic right of players to freedom of movement. In particular, even within contract, players gained the right to transfer, subject to reasonable remuneration for the loss suffered by the selling club, which was settled by forced arbitration if the two clubs could not agree.

This introduced the possibility of competition between clubs to attract star players, with obvious benefits to these players in terms of remuneration. However, up until the present day, the clubs retained ownership of the registration even when the player's contract expired, and they therefore maintained the right to compensation when a player was transferred (even out of contract). The right of clubs to retain and trade players' registrations when out of contract has now been overturned following a recent challenge in the European Court by a Belgian player Marc Bosman. The Court's judgement at the end of 1995 effectively withdrew any ownership rights of clubs over players or their activities, which is no more than the situation for any employee in any business. However, it has taken a long time for football players to reach this stage.

Since the abolition of the maximum wage and the 'retain and transfer' system players have been in a position to negotiate deals on their own behalf. Within contract, players have been able to bargain for higher wages against the threat that they will demand a transfer. Once their contracts expired, they could sell themselves to the highest bidder regardless of the views of the club (because the club could not refuse to sell the registration). Within contract transfers depended on the willingness of the club holding the registration to sell, but if agreement could not be reached a system of compulsory arbitration enforced a settlement.

Most commentators agree that the transfer system has become a murky world of secret deals and backhanders[4]. It follows that this murkiness carries over to the pay setting of players. Deals involve the club owners, the team managers, agents acting on behalf of the players, agents acting on behalf of the clubs (against League rules), as well as the players themselves. Managers, despite being only salaried employees of the club, exercise a strong influence of these deals and in more than one case in the recent past have been found to be lining their own pockets.

The system of pay determination lacks transparency[5] and clubs are under no obligations to reveal data. It is well known that the sums discussed in the newspapers are mostly speculative and are often wide of the mark[6]. The only other source of data is the accounts of the clubs which must reveal the total wage bill, but not individual data.

But is it procedurally unfair? The fundamental point here is that the player is in a position to negotiate his salary with anyone willing to pay his wages. Thus there is a clearly defined buyer and seller, whatever intermediaries either of the parties choose to introduce. Unlike the case of company directors, there is a well defined set of persons who constitute 'the buyer' and players are not in a position to contribute to the decision making process of the buyer in any other capacity.

Market Efficiency

Directors

In general terms a labour market may be deemed efficient if the rate of pay offered for the job brings into balance the supply and demand for labour[7]. At the offered wage rate there should be no excess supply or excess demand. Now, whilst it is obviously true that there would be long queues for interview if any large corporation opened up the competition to fill a board level post at current rates of pay, this does not necessarily imply that there is excess supply. To meet their demand each company requires a supply of (a) suitably qualified individuals with experience relevant to that businesss need and (b) effort on the job from those individuals. 'Effort' in this sense means more than simply long hours. It means applying the right sort of commitment to the success of the firm, using whatever criteria the firm adopts to judge success[8].

Researchers on director compensation have tended to focus very specifically on the issue effort supply. The problem of effort supply arises for two reasons. Firstly, the considerable variability in any objective set for the director (e.g. share price performance) makes it inappropriate for the director to be rewarded simply in proportion to the objective, to the extent that this variability is beyond the control of the director. What the director would prefer, like any employee, is an insurance policy against large variations of income (particularly in cases where outcomes involve large losses)[9]. An efficient solution to this first problem would be set a fixed wage in return for an agreed level of effort, but only if effort is observable. But that is the second problem, effort is rarely observable. A promise to pay a fixed wage when effort is unobservable is inefficient because the director has no incentive to supply any effort at all. The unobservability of effort is a particularly acute problem for company directors. Consider two directors from different companies watching a game of football together from an executive box. Are they cutting an important deal or just enjoying the football? There seems to be no method by which an independent observer could ever hope to answer this question satisfactorily.

The efficient solution to the effort supply problem when faced with these problems (risk aversion and effort unobservability) is for the company owners to write a contract paying the director a fixed basic wage and a bonus proportional to the performance of the company[10]. The base wage provides insurance, and the variable bonus provides incentives.

This theoretical result has led researchers to focus on the pay-performance link. To test for efficiency in practice means selecting a sample of directors and estimating the statistical relationship between annual pay and the annual performance of the company. The estimated coefficient for the performance indicator represents the sensitivity of pay to performance. Generally, a positive coefficient confirms the theoretical prediction. At first blush this might seem like a rather odd way to research executive pay. First, in almost all cases we know that directors do have base salary and bonus packages and therefore there seems no need to demonstrate that they exist through the statistical analysis. However, we also know that salaries are revised from year to year, and so in practice there may be cases where actual payments increase over time even when company performance is moving in the opposite direction. Second, the theory only states that there should be a positive relationship, but it does not say how great it should be. It is thus a rather weak test of market efficiency. Third, unless there are a great many annual observations of each individual director (and in practice there are seldom more than ten) it is only feasible to estimate an average relationship across individuals, rather than a person-specific relationship, which is what is suggested by the theory[11]. Fourth, this is only efficiency in one sense, namely that directors get the right sort of incentives to supply effort. It says nothing, for example, about whether the absolute level of pay is appropriate.

There are a great many empirical studies on this issue[12], which all reach more or less the same conclusion: there is a small but statistically significant positive relationship between executive pay and performance. This finding has been trenchantly stated by Jensen and Murphy (1990). They argued that while the relationship has the right sign and therefore confirms the theory, the relationship is much smaller than might be expected. For example, they point out that, for their sample of executives, a $1000 increase in the value of an executive's company will lead to a mere $3.25 increase in pay[13]. However, this statement is hard to interpret since the theory does not tell us just how sensitive pay should be to be efficient. Without some view on the degree of risk aversion of executives and the choices that they face a proper judgement is not possible. In a recent paper Haubrich (1994) showed that the Jensen and Murphy estimates might be efficient given some plausible assumptions about the executives and their environment. There is also a presentational aspect of the Jensen and Murphy results which may be misleading. The sensitivity of pay to total shareholder value is very small because executive pay is measured in hundreds of thousands (of dollars) and because share-holder value is measured in billions (of dollars). To get a high sensitivity executives would have to be paid salaries dimensionally similar to shareholder value. Indeed, this may be what Jensen and Murphy believe is ideal, however, it can at least be argued that such large payments would not be warranted by the contribution of the board of directors. If the relationship between executive pay and performance is measured as an elasticity, that is the percentage increase in pay caused by a 1% increase in shareholder value, then in practice the estimates appear to be around the plausible sounding 1% mark. Unfortunately, Jensen and Murphy do not quote these figures, but estimates for the UK based on the widest currently available measures of pay suggest elasticities in the region of 0.8 to 1.5[14].

However, even if directors' pay setting is efficient in the sense of ensuring optimal effort supply, this does not imply that wages are efficient in a general sense. Indeed, there is some straightforward evidence that pay levels are higher than theoretical efficiency requires. If pay is set in order to overcome the effort elicitation problem, there will be a balance between incentive pay and base pay. The total (expected) salary should be sufficient to prevent the director moving elsewhere, but no more. Now, we know that salaries have increased significantly over the last decade and a half. For example, in their sample Gregg et al. (1994) find that the median base salary plus ordinary bonuses for FT500 named directors increased by 98% in real terms, and total pay increased by 144% over the period 1982–1991. The theory suggests that as incomes increase, so does the tolerance for risk and therefore the greater the proportion of income which individuals would be willing to take in the form of perform- ance pay. In effect, richer employees demand less insurance, and so the owners can offer greater incentives, which should in turn lead to better performance. Efficient contracts would allow rising sensitivity of pay to performance as incomes increases.

In fact, Gregg et al. (1994) find that there was no significant increase in the sensitivity of directors' pay to performance throughout the 1980s. Despite the increasing significance of incentive components such as share options, the sensitivity of total pay to performance was unchanged, suggesting that base pay was being used to smooth out any increased volatility caused by perform- ance related pay components. Since there appears to be no other market factor which can account for the growth of pay in the 1980s, the increases appear to be have been driven by forces other than market efficiency.

Another aspect of efficiency can be considered by looking at the turnover of directors. The problem here is finding an unambiguous test. For example, it might be expected that poor performance will lead not merely to lower remuneration but ultimately to dismissal, voluntarily or involuntarily. How- ever, how much turnover is efficient? In practice there is very little among directors in the UK (Gregg et al.), and somewhat more in the US (Jensen and Murphy). In particular, Gregg et al. (1994) found that poor company perform- ance in terms of shareholder returns had no significant effect on the probability of leaving the job immediately, or in the ultimate length of tenure. More generally, it is sometimes claimed that directors must be paid well in order to prevent them moving from one job to another. Whilst it is true that lower down the executive ladder there is a certain amount of movement, it is rare in the UK for a director to move to another company. In fact, most board directors have worked a considerable length of time in the same company and hold their board position until retirement. This does not prove that high pay is inefficient, since it can be claimed that it is the high pay that is keeping turnover down to very low levels. However, it is a common feeling that at 10% salary cut for an director paid £500,000 per year would not induce that person to quit. More research into this issue is required.

Thus, whilst conventional research has tended to support a very limited notion of market efficiency in directors' pay setting (ensuring effort supply), once the search is widened to examine market efficiency in general there is little evidence to support the notion of an efficient market. Partly this reflects the peculiar focus of research and the lack of knowledge of internal company processes. However, the findings of Gregg et al. relating to the probability of director turnover and the absence of increasing pay/performance sensitivity when pay levels increase are hard to reconcile with the notion of an efficient market[15]. More work remains to be done in this area.

Footballers

For footballers there is no effort observability problem. The employer can observe the performance of the player on at least forty occasions in an eight month period plus any Cup competition games. Not only this, but if the employer is any doubt as to the accuracy of his observations, he can, on most Saturday afternoons, consult up to thirty thousand witnesses for their opinions[16] (not to mention rerunning the video). It is therefore relatively easy to assess the contribution of the players, both in terms of effort and ability[17].

For professional footballers, ability varies much more than effort. In order to play at all a minimum level of effort is required, but in general most players would expect to apply close to their best efforts most of the time. It is certainly not the case that higher pay levels are expected to elicit significantly higher effort levels and in general incentive pay plays a relatively small role in the compensation of footballers. Variations in pay have much more to do with the variance in ability, which is both considerable and observable. The variance of ability is the main difference between winning and losing in football. In practice, professional footballers are an undisputed elite. Very few serious followers of the game would suggest that they could even remotely reach the levels of performance achieved by professionals. Indeed, annually, gifted amateurs have the opportunity to pitch themselves against the professional through the FA Cup. In practice, amateurs seldom make any headway even against the lowliest professional teams. The fact that ability and effort are so readily observable guarantees efficiency in the sense that the hierarchy of players in the League is indeed an accurate reflection of the hierarchy of talents.

This observability is the basis of active trading in the market for the talents of professional footballers. It is rare for a player to stay at the same club for his entire career (unless the career is very short) while five or more moves in a ten-year playing career are not uncommon. Footballers are traded, partly, because their talents are transparent and therefore can be easily valued. On this basis the market for footballers can be compared to the notion of an efficient financial market, where the assets which are traded are players' talents, rather than company shares or some other financial instrument. A textbook definition of an efficient financial market is a market in which 'information is widely and cheaply available to investors and that all relevant and ascertainable information is already reflected in security prices' (Brealey and Myers (1988: 282). For 'security prices', substitute 'the cost of acquiring a particular playing talent'. Investors, in this case, are football clubs. At the very top of the profession the market is relatively thin: there are relatively few extraordinary talents and relatively few clubs which can afford to buy them. However, taking the market as a whole, there are a large enough number of buyers and sellers to ensure that the market can operate efficiently.

There is a very close analogy between player prices and stock prices. For well known companies or players it is almost impossible to get a bargain because so much is already known. For example, investors can easily put a value on IBM shares and clubs can easily name the market price for a well known talent such as Paul Gascoigne. On the other hand, small emerging companies or emerging playing talent can sometimes be snapped up cheaply, because only real specialists can invest in the expensive and time consuming business of talent scouting. The clearest evidence that the market for football players is efficient can be obtained by relating the cost of players to the performance of the team, measured in terms of League position achieved. A simple statistical relationship of League position as a function of the annual wage bill of a club relative to the average of all other clubs yields a goodness-of-fit measure (R^2) of 0.70[18]. That is, 70% of the variation of position can be accounted for by relative spending on wages. This relationship can only be this strong because spending does indeed translate into relative outperformance[19]. By contrast the regression of share price performance on directors' salaries yields an R^2 of only about 2%. One feature of the relationship described here is that wage data alone are a more accurate predictor of club position than the sum of wage and transfer spending. That is because transfer spending represent gambles based on the expected development and fitness of players. In most cases, wages are only paid out by the clubs if players actually perform[20].

In fact, this view of the market for footballers' talents is similar to that held for all sports (e.g. Fort and Quirk (1995)). Sports markets are efficient in the sense that relative payments reflect relative talents. However, there is no doubt that the absolute level of salaries has increased substantially in recent years. For example, between 1974 and 1994, real wages more than doubled on average in the sample of clubs described above. Much of this may have to do with the legacy of low pay left over from the underpayment of players in the past. At the very bottom of the professional ladder, salaries still reflect the opportunity cost of the individual player which is most commonly manual employment. Consider Scunthorpe United which in the 1992/3 season came 14th in the new Third Division (84 places below the Premier League Champions), close to the bottom of the professional pile. The club spent £666,000 on salaries in that year. Supposing that this was divided among thirty employees (including the Manager, full squad and a small administrative staff) and that salary overheads were 25% of the total. In that case the before-tax take-home pay of a player would have been about £320 per week, or about £240 per week after tax. According to the New Earnings Survey, full-time manual male wages in 1993 were £278 per week in the Scunthorpe area.

It would appear that there is an efficient market for professional players in the sense that:

(a)   Information about talent is cheaply and widely available.
(b)   Trading is frequent.
(c)   There are enough buyers and sellers to ensure that neither side of the market possesses monopoly power.

Distributive fairness

How can the chairman of a multinational corporation be compared to a professional footballer, a roadsweeper or a nurse? To make judgements about the fairness of salary levels through such comparisons is to make judgements about what is and is not valuable. This immediately begs the question, valuable to whom: to oneself, to one's family, to one's community, to one's country, to the world? This can be a dangerous game, particularly if one is prepared to impose one's judgements on others. It is perfectly feasible to say that relative rewards are unfair but that nothing can be done about it. During the heated debate on the subject of top executive pay in recent years this appears to be precisely the position held by the British Government, at least until the promise was made to provide legislation, if necessary, to back up the recommendations of the Greenbury Committee. However, such a non-interventionist position, while intellectually respectable, seems to carry little public support. For those who would intervene, in most cases the recommended route is government legislation. The problem with legislating for directors' pay is that the picking on directors alone seems arbitrary (why not other instances which are per-ceived to be unfair?). A general policy on the redistribution of wealth through penal taxation of high incomes would certainly achieve the end of reducing the rewards to directors, but squeezing the rich in general remains (at present) a much less popular prescription.

One might have thought that directors, criticised for the size of their remuneration compared to other potentially worthy citizens, might steer clear of the discussion on distributive fairness. However, the introductory quote from Iain Vallance, Chairman of British Telecom, illustrates that this is not necessarily the case. He argues that executive remuneration is at least as justified as the pay of footballers, pop stars, lottery winners, accountants or lawyers. It would indeed be an interesting experiment to ask the general public whose salary they thought more justifiable, the Premier League's leading goalscorer or the chairman of the most profitable company in the FT30. Mr Vallance seems to believe that the activities of corporate chairmen are more important than the activities of entertainers. However, even if, as Mr Vallance seems to imply, the economy would collapse without the contribution of the senior executives, this weighting seems to underestimate the very real psychic pleasures derived by consumers from the performances of top entertainers. Mr Vallance may personally prefer, say, 5% growth in BT profits to Manchester United[21] winning the League, by why should this be a general preference? In the end, Mr Vallance may consider society's priorities odd, but then society may not be entirely at ease with Mr Vallance's.

Some implications of the Greenbury Report

The Greenbury Report set out to respond to public concerns about directors' remuneration. In particular, the Committee identified pay increases and share option grants to directors in recently privatised utilities as being the focus of concern. The Committee was set up by the CBI and of its eleven members, a majority were company chairman. Of the ninety two persons or organisations who are listed as contributing to the Committee sixty one (that is, two thirds) were themselves company directors (mostly chairmen).

The Greenbury Report outlined a code of best practice for all directors and suggested that in particular privatised utilities should exercise restraint in awarding pay increases to directors. The Report therefore appeared to use direct criticism of the privatised utilities as a way of drawing fire from the question of directors' pay in general. Apart from being convenient for the majority of directors, this did appear to reflect a genuine public concern. However, here we will consider the basic recommendations of the code and interpret them in terms of the three concepts of fairness discussed in the paper.

The principal recommendations of the Greenbury Code are:

1.   Remuneration Committees composed exclusively of non-executive directors directly accountable to shareholders should fix the remuneration of directors. The Committee should consult the chairman and professionals inside and outside the company.

2.   The Committee should make public the company policy on directors' remuneration. The report should contain details of directors' pay on an individual basis. It should contain details on all elements of remuneration, including all facts relating to share options and pension contributions.

3.   The remuneration package should be designed so as to 'attract, retain and motivate directors'. Incentives should align the interests of directors and shareholders but longer term schemes other than share options should be considered, including performance criteria other than the simple share price. In general a wide range of schemes should be considered.

4.   Notice periods in service contracts should generally be no more than one year in length and should be explicitly justified where longer.

5.   Long term incentive schemes (of duration greater than one year) should be voted on at the Annual General Meeting.

To a large extent, these recommendations endorsed those of the earlier Cadbury Report on corporate governance, but in some particulars went well beyond Cadbury. Some recommendations were trailed in advance and reflected widely held views, for example the reduction in notice periods to a single year. However, some recommendations have provoked fierce resistance from directors, in particular the requirement to reveal pension contributions. Full implementation of the Greenbury Code would affect all the aspects of fairness and efficiency discussed above. A version of the code will be made compulsory by the London Stock Exchange for all listed companies[22].

First, from the point of view of procedural fairness, the aim of the Code is to create as great a distance as possible between directors and the decisions relating to their remuneration package. The proposals go as far as it is possible to go while preserving the absolute right of a company to set its own pay policies. However, given the problem that directors possess influence, whatever the rules say, the Greenbury Code is unlikely to put an end to claims of director manipulation. Are there any alternatives which could deal with this problem? One radical alternative would be for companies to delegate some of their powers to set pay. For example, a salary cap could be fixed by an independent committee created to arbitrate pay awards within a group (or club) of companies. Such a committee could fix a total allowable annual spend for board salaries, while allowing individual companies to determine individual director pay and the structure of executive pay within the confines of the committee's ceiling. As long as enough companies subscribed to the scheme, the committee could be reasonably considered to be independent of influence from any one board of directors. Salary cap schemes have operated intermittently in various professional sports leagues in the UK and US since the last century. In practice most of them have been abolished because they held down the pay of valued professionals (although no one ever suggested they adversely affected the performance of players). Since the recent escalation of directors' pay is seen as part of the problem, it would be some years at least before this became an issue.

Secondly, in terms of market efficiency, the main contribution of the Greenbury Code is to promote improved performance measures for use in setting incentive pay. In general terms the report has little to say about efficiency and, remarkably enough, it said nothing at all about the historic relationship between directors' pay and performance, despite the voluminous literature on the subject that has been referred to above. The report says, rather lamely: 'There is a market for executive talent . . . However, the market is imperfect.' In practice, as discussed above, there is very little movement of directors between companies and very little evidence to support the notion of market efficiency. What is clear is that relying on performance indicators other the share price is likely to drive a bigger wedge between pay and performance. As far as shareholders are concerned, performance is the return on investment measured by share price appreciation plus dividends. It is not performance relative to other companies. For example, if an investor in Shell loses 5% on his investment, he is no better off for knowing that BPs investors lost 10%, nor is he worse off for knowing that BPs return was 40% when Shell's was 20%. Proper incentive alignment (to solve the effort elicitation problem) means ensuring that the employee (director) and the employer (shareholder) share the same goal. There is no evidence whatsoever that there exists any indicator which is a good predictor of future share prices[23]. Indeed, there is considerable danger in using alternative performance measures if these start to involve manipulable data such as accounting information. In terms of market efficiency, therefore, Greenbury appears to be a step backwards.

Finally, in terms of distributive fairness, Greenbury uses the utilities to draw fire. Specifically the report says 'there is little doubt that the remuneration committees of a number of companies in the privatised water and energy sectors have developed, perhaps unintentionally, remuneration packages richer than is required to recruit, retain and motivate quality managers'. While this comment seems to reflect a concern with efficiency, it is clear from the section on remuneration policy in general that distributive concerns were weighted equally with efficiency concerns. The only specific comparison which the Committee was willing to make for directors as a group was with their international colleagues. This must be taken as a comment on distributive fairness rather than efficiency since in practice there is virtually no international movement into or out of the UK at director level. Thus the Committee argued that:

(a)   Remuneration levels are mostly within the average of European practice and well below American levels.
(b)   Disclosure is at a much higher level in the UK than in other European countries.
(c)   Performance related elements are much greater in the US but tend to be smaller in other European countries.
(d)   The ratio of highest to lowest salaries within companies was comparable to the average of other European countries.

In practice, international comparisons are unlikely to carry much weight when observers make distributive judgements. For example, if a minimum wage were set in the UK by a future Labour government, the equivalent rate in the US or in France would probably not enter into most people's judgements, despite the similarities with both countries and their long experience of minimum wages. In practice, what counts for fairness are people perceived to be in the same society and, rightly or wrongly, societies are nowadays characterised by national boundaries. Greenbury fails to confront such national concerns.

Some conclusions

By evaluating pay setting in terms of procedural fairness, market efficiency and distributive fairness, this paper has considered the similarities and differences between the remuneration of professional footballers and company directors. The main differences stressed in this paper relate to procedures and to the operation of the market for talent.

The perception of procedural defects in the setting of directors' pay has been at the heart of much of the controversy. Whilst much has been done through the Cadbury and Greenbury Reports to ensure that directors are distanced (and seen to be distanced) from the process of setting their own salary, there will inevitably remain a suspicion of undue influence, given the powerful positions held by these individuals. One suggestion floated in the paper is that an independent board fixes boardroom pay settlements for individual companies within a group of companies, in the same way as salary caps have been fixed in professional team sports leagues, both in the UK and in the US. The merit of such a proposal lies in clearly breaking (or significantly diminishing) the link between pay setting and executive influence inside the corporation.

Problems of procedure are much less controversial with respect to the pay setting of professional footballers (even though procedures are widely seen as corrupt) because it is generally recognised that there is a functioning market for the talent of players. In football, talent is readily transferable and issues such as effort and incentives do not pose a problem. Although at the upper end of the market there are relatively few buyers and sellers, overall the market for footballing talent corresponds quite closely to the notion of an efficient market.

Identifying talent and effort are much greater problems in the case of directors. Because of this there is really no such thing as a market for directors. Buyers find it very hard to put a value on what they are buying, and can do little to observe what they get for what they pay. Few directors in practice move from one company to another. As a result there is little discipline in pay setting, and huge variations are both possible and observed in practice. Reports such as Greenbury, whilst welcome if they produce more information on pay setting and the actual size of directors' remuneration, can do little to change the fundamental problems associated with the absence of a proper market for the services of directors.

Finally, the issue of distributive fairness will always be controversial. Directors of public corporations may consider themselves unlucky, being forced to reveal their salary levels while similar types of professionals such as bankers, lawyers and accountants maintain their confidentiality. However, in order to placate a jealous public, perhaps directors should spend more time explaining to the public exactly what they do.

This paper has dealt with the notion of fairness. It has lent some support to the view that directors' pay levels and remuneration packages are unfair, even when compared to other highly paid groups. But even if it is accepted that directors' pay levels are unfair, is there much that can be done about it? This paper has suggested an administrative solution through a process of setting salary caps. While a solution such as this may be prone to evasion and distortion, it would certainly act as a brake on the rate of pay increases.

Notes

1. An early UK study based on this data was Meeks and Whittington (1975).
2. Even though such practices may have been widespread. there were always some constraints. First, salary consultants may have dampened expectations somewhat (although the contrary argument is sometimes presented). Second, non-executive directors may have added a note of independent caution to discussion of company pay. This too is a controversial point, since non-executives usually have executive directors to thank for their appointment, a position which typically carries some status. Studies such as Cosh and Hughes (1987) have also shown that there is a good deal of cross-representation on company boards, which may introduce an element of reciprocity into the pay setting process.
3. See Fort and Quirk (1995) for a survey on the US and Cairns, Jennett and Sloane (1986) for a survey with a UK slant.
4. For some fascinating examples see Fynn and Guest (1994), Chapter 10.
5. Although the PFA does keep records on behalf of players and has allowed

researchers access to the data in the past, see for example Carmichael and Thomas (1992).

6. See Crick and Smith (1989: 230–235) for some accurate transfer data for the case of Manchester United over a forty year period.

7. This is obviously a simplification. Supply and demand may themselves be distorted by factors which render a labour market equilibrium inefficient from a more general perspective. Furthermore, externalities (real effects not captured by market prices) may also create inefficiencies. However, for the purposes of this discussion the simplification is not a problem.

8. In practice this is likely to be the long term value of the shares which the owners hold.

9. Only if directors were indifferent to risk would it make sense to tie their pay entirely to highly variable objectives such as share prices.

10. The precise derivation of this result is tricky. Whilst it is easy to derive if very simple functional forms are chosen for the characterisation of risk and the utility of the executive, there exist some specifications for which the result will not hold. See Tirole (1988: 51–55) for a general discussion of the problem. However, the intuition is so strong, and range of cases for which the result holds is so large, that most economists appear to accept its generality.

11. Smith and Szymanski (1995) found a very different relationship estimated by the average of time series regressions for individuals compared with cross section estimates.

12. Clark and Main in this volume provide a more comprehensive set of references. The most important recent contributions are Jensen and Murphy (1990), and Gibbons and Murphy (1992) for the US. In the UK the most detailed work on pay performance sensitivity has been carried out by Main et al. (1996) and Gregg et al. (1994).

13. In the paper there are many different estimates depending on a number of different measures they use. However, this one is their preferred estimate.

14. The 0.8 is taken from Gregg, Machin and Szymanski (1994) who use a crude measure of share option values; 1.5 is taken from Main, Bruce and Buck (1996) who use a much more accurate measure of option values on a smaller sample.

15. There are some other studies which adopt slightly different approaches to market efficiency. Main, O'Reilly and Wade (1993) are motivated by the theoretical literature on labour tournaments (e.g. Lazear and Rosen (1981) to examine the effect of board remuneration as an incentive device for employees lower down the executive ladder). Gibbons and Murphy (1992) examine the relationship between executive pay and performance to take into account the fact that in the early part of their careers employees do not need direct financial incentives as much as in the later part of their careers, because early on they are willing to make extra effort in order to build up a good reputation and so gain larger rewards in the future.

16. In practice, consultation is normally restricted to the chorus of comments shouted from the terraces. The message is usually unmistakable.
17. To football fans this might seem an odd proposition, since the ability of a player is often a hotly disputed topic and opinions seem to vary hugely. However, this stems from the hyperbole which is a consequence of the passions provoked by the game, and the fact that very small differences in skill can have very large consequences.
18. For a sample of 35 English Football League clubs 1974–1993 (including the first year of the Premier League), a regression of the natural logarithm of position (counting first place in the first division as one, first place in the second division as 23 and so on, ignoring the change in names brought about by the Premier League) on the logarithm of wage bill relative to the average wage bill of the 35 clubs in that year, yields a coefficient of -1.34 with a t-statistic of 41.84 and an adjusted R^2 of 0.715.
19. This relationship was considered in more detail of Szymanski and Smith (1995) who used a dataset of 48 clubs over 16 years. Exogeneity tests for the wage variable were passed, implying that causation pointed in the correct direction i.e. from wages to performance.
20. Although clubs may guarantee payments by insuring players for health risks.
21. Although according to the Financial Times, Sir Richard Greenbury is a passionate Manchester United supporter.
22. At the time of writing the final version was still being negotiated, but it seems clear that the original recommendations will remain substantially intact.
23. Such information would immediately be used by investors, automatically influencing the share price: efficient markets use all information instantly.

References

Brealey, R. and Myers, S, 1988. *Principles of Corporate Finance*. Third Edition. McGraw Hill.

Cadbury, A., 1992. *The Financial Aspects of Corporate Governance: The Code of Best Practice*. London: Professional Publishing Ltd.

Cairns, J., Jennett, N. and Sloane, P., 1986. The Economics of Professional Team Sports: a survey of theory and evidence. *Journal of Economic Studies* 13, 1–80.

Carmichael, F. and Thomas, D., 1992. Bargaining in the Transfer Market: Theory and Evidence, University of Aberystwyth mimeo.

Conyon, M., 1994. Corporate Governance Changes in UK Companies Between 1988 and 1993. *Corporate Governance* 2, 87–99.

Cosh, A. and Hughes, A., 1987. The Anatomy of Corporate Control: Directors, Shareholders and Executive Remuneration in Giant US and UK Companies. *Cambridge Journal of Economics* 11, 285–313.

Crick, M. and Smith, D., 1989. *The Betrayal of a Legend*. London: Pelham Books.

Fort, R. and Quirk, J., 1995. Cross-subsidisation, Incentives, and Outcomes in Professional Team Sports. *Journal of Economic Literature* 33, 1265–1299.

Fynn, A. and Guest, L., 1994. *Out of Time: Why Football Isn't Working*. London: Simon and Schuster.

Gregg, P., Machin, S. and Szymanski, S., 1994. The Compensation of Top Directors of UK Companies. Paper presented at the 1994 American Economic Association Conference.

Gibbons, R. and Murphy, K., 1992. Optimal incentive contracts in the presence of career concerns: theory and evidence. *Journal of Political Economy* **100**, 468–505.

Haubrich, J., 1994. Risk Aversion, Performance Pay, and the Principal-Agent Problem. *Journal of Political Economy* **102**, 258–276.

Jenkinson, T. and Mayer, C., 1992. The assessment: Corporate Governance and Corporate Control. *Oxford Review of Economic Policy* **8**, 1–10.

Jensen, M. and Murphy, K., 1990. Performance pay and top management incentives. *Journal of Political Economy* **98**, 225–264.

Lazear, E. and Rosen, S., 1981. Rank-Order Tournaments as Optimum Labour Contracts. *Journal of Political Economy* **89**, 841–864.

Main, B.G.M., 1993. Pay in the boardroom: Practices and Procedures. *Personnel Review* **22**, 1–14.

Main, B.G.M., 1994. The Nomination Process and Corporate Governance, A Missing Link. *Corporate Governance* **2**, 165–73.

Main, B., Bruce, A. and Buck, T., 1996. Total Board Remuneration and Company Performance. *Economic Journal,* forthcoming.

Main, B., O'Reilly, C. and Wade, J., 1993. Top Executive Pay: Tournament or Teamwork. *Journal of Labour Economics* **11**, 606–628.

Smith, A., 1981. *An Inquiry into the Nature and Causes of the Wealth of Nations.* Indianapolis: Liberty Press.

Smith, R. and Szymanski, S., 1995. Executive Pay and Performance: the empirical importance of the participation constraint, *International Journal of the Economics of Business,* **2**, 485–495.

Szymanski, S. and Smith, R., 1995. The English football industry: Profit, performance and industrial structure. London Business School mimeo.

The Study Group on Directors Remuneration, 1995. *Directors Remuneration: Report of a Study Group Chaired by Sir Richard Greenbury.* London: Gee Publishing.

Tirole, Jean, 1988. *The Theory of Industrial Organization.* Cambridge (Mass.): MIT Press.

Walvin, J., 1994. *The Peoples' Game: The History of Football Revisited.* Edinburgh: Mainstream Publishing.

The Governance of Remuneration for Senior Executives: making use of options

Simon J. Clark and Brian G. M. Main

Introduction

The issue of corporate governance in the UK assumed its current level of prominence following certain spectacular company failures such as Coloroll and Polly Peck. The impression was gained that in these and other instances the companies in general, and the shareholders in particular, had been poorly served by the supervisory mechanisms of board oversight and external audit. One direct and visible consequence of the concern that these events evoked was the Cadbury Committee (1992).

Furthermore, around the same time, a general consensus was emerging in the popular press and elsewhere that top executive pay was in some sense 'out of control' and could be taken as yet another sign of a breakdown of governance in British companies. Pay at the top of a company is a matter of public record. It is, therefore, an apparently straightforward matter for outsiders to gauge the extent to which the top executives are being rewarded for good company performance and punished for poor performance. If the alignment of the executive's pay outcome and company's performance is regarded as providing an incentive effect that addresses the low level of direct or close managerial supervision to which top executives are subject – as a consequence of the separation of ownership and control – then this relationship can be taken as one indicator of the quality of a company's corporate governance[1].

In the event, the Cadbury Report (1992) went into some considerable detail regarding what it saw as 'good practice' in the matter of determining executive pay, although executive pay as such was not explicitly mentioned in the Committee's terms of reference. The pay guidelines contained in the Cadbury Report involve the utilisation of remuneration committees, participation by independent directors in the pay determination process and fuller disclosure of the basis on which executive pay is determined in a company. But the pay debate continues unabated, fuelled by publicity given to large pay awards in the recently privatised public utilities such as electricity, gas and water. Early in 1995 the CBI, at the Government's prodding, set up the Greenbury Committee specifically to examine the subject. Its Report and Code of Best Practice can be seen as a strengthening of the Cadbury Code.

As will be discussed below, most empirical studies find only a modest connection between top executive pay and company performance. This has been taken by many as implying that governance procedures should be strengthened along the lines of Cadbury and Greenbury, in terms of remuneration, committee membership and reporting – with special importance being laid on the role of the non-executive directors. But to a large extent such recommendations ignore the 'social psychology' involved in boardroom relations within the context of a unitary board. These effects influence and condition the decisions of the non-executives in the light of each director's personal circumstances and his/her personal relationships with other board members. This is a far cry from the independent rational decision makers implicitly envisioned in some of the codes of non-executive behaviour. Details of these effects are spelled out below.

Because such 'social influence' effects tend to undermine the implementation of any incentive devices that rely upon discretion or assessment by the non-executive directors, this then places a premium on incentives that are more mechanistic, in the sense of relying on outside effects and not depending on interpretation or judgement by non-executives. Incentive mechanisms such as the award of share options offer a degree of objectivity that should promise them a major role in the design of executive pay packages. Unfortunately the current regulatory environment (primarily operating through the Share Incentive Scheme Guidelines of the Association of British Insurers) puts a limit on the extent to which this is possible. The situation is not helped by the current reporting practices of the accounting profession in the area of executive share options. Finally, there are some widespread misperceptions regarding the relative effectiveness of share versus option that cloud the issue, and seem to have led the Greenbury Committee to adopt an unsympathetic view of executive share options.

The paper concludes by offering some policy recommendations regarding the role of institutional shareholders in the governance of aspects of executive pay design, and in the setting of executive incentives more generally. These depend, to no small extent, upon an improvement in the way that accountants in the UK report and recognise executive share options.

Empirical studies

This is an area where the empirical work in the USA has led that in the UK. Studies of the empirical relationship between top executive pay and company performance have a long history in the USA, going back to Roberts (1956). Originally focused on the relative importance of profits versus size (e.g., see Lewellen and Huntsman (1970)), this part of the literature has been summarised by Rosen (1992: 185) as 'something of an empirical zoo', a phrase worth bearing in mind when considering all work in this area. Later work, best dated from Murphy (1985), moved to a more overtly principal-agent framework and the impressive range of contributions that followed are reviewed in Rosen (1992).

Jensen and Murphy (1990a) is widely accepted as the highpoint of this work. It is in this paper that there appears the much cited pay-performance statistic of $3.25 increase in chief executive officer (CEO) wealth for every $1,000 increase in shareholder wealth, a result summarised as 'inconsistent with the implications of formal agency models of optimal contracting' (Jensen and Murphy (1990a: 227)).

Work in the UK has followed a similar pattern[2], although labouring with more limited data owing to the lower standard of disclosure requirements that apply in the UK. Most of this work has been recently summarised in Conyon, Gregg and Machin (1995). There, UK results are shown to be broadly consistent with the Jensen and Murphy benchmark and widely judged to suggest a surprisingly low pay-performance relationship at the top of large companies. These findings change when the analysis is broadened to include the effects of deferred components of pay such as share options (see Gregg, Machin and Szymanski (1993b) and Main, Buck and Bruce (1996)), when the pay-performance connection is much strengthened[3].

In terms of the impact of governance arrangements on the level and composition of top executive pay, there has been remarkably little work in the UK. In a cross-sectional study, Main and Johnston (1993) suggest that the operation of a remuneration committee[4] (a principal component of the Cadbury guidelines) could be associated with higher levels of executive remuneration, by some 17 per cent, and that pay was no more incentive-oriented with a remuneration committee than without. Conyon (1994b) finds that, in a longitudinal sample of 214 large UK companies, the use of remuneration committees had increased from 54 per cent in 1988 to 94 per cent in 1993. Furthermore, he estimates that adoption of a remuneration committee is associated with a 2 per cent reduction in the level of the CEO's pay. While empirically modest, this is a statistically significant result.

In the following section of the paper we will look more closely at the impact of internal governance arrangements on executive pay awards.

Social Influence in the Boardroom

There have been several reactions to the findings outlined above concerning what is generally regarded as the weak relationship between top executive pay and company performance. Some claim that such empirical results do not, in fact, invalidate the view that an adequate pay-based solution to the principal-agent problem is in place at the top of large companies. Others offer alternative interpretations of the theory that may be more consistent with the observed facts. Finally, the pragmatists call for recognition that current arrangements are flawed and suggest changes to current practice.

Papers by Garen (1994) and by Haubrich (1994) are representative of the first view. Haubrich demonstrates that, within the context of the principal-agent model and with certain assumptions regarding parameter values, a pay-performance connection of $10 pay for every $1,000 of additional shareholder value would certainly represent a satisfactory arrangement and that even markedly smaller pay-performance results would emerge given alternative assumptions regarding parameter values (risk aversion, disutility of effort, etc.). Garen (1994) suggests that a direct test of principal-agent theory along the lines of Jensen and Murphy (1990a) is not practicable owing to the large number of unknowns, and offers a more realisable test in terms of the comparative statics of the model. He argues that the results of Jensen and Murphy (1990b) can be seen as offering supportive evidence of principal-agent mechanisms at work.

The second reaction is to suggest a reinterpretation of the theory that does not sit so uncomfortably with the facts. Tournament theory as outlined by Lazear and Rosen (1981) can be viewed in this light. If the current pay of the top executive represents the prize in some rank-order tournament that has been played out among a cohort of executives, then the current level of CEO pay need no longer reflect contemporaneous productivity. While divorced from current productivity, the top executive's pay award can still serve the ends of economic efficiency by providing visible proof of the existence of a 'prize' and enforcing the incentive for the next cohort of aspiring CEOs to align their efforts with the interests of the company in order to out-compete fellow executives in performance, and hence win the prize (the CEO job and pay)[5].

The third response to the Jensen and Murphy (1990a) type of finding is of the 'what else did you expect?' variety, and suggests changing the way things are done (see Murphy (1994)). Given the unitary board structure that applies to the UK and US firms under discussion here, and with the nominations process in the UK until recently largely in the hands of the chairman[6] (Main 1994b), it would be unwise to overlook the small group dynamics that arise in such situations. In a recent review of the possibility of moving to two-tier board structures in the UK, Owen (1995) stresses the firm hold that the unitary board structure has in the UK. Owen highlights the critical comments made by Sir Owen Green regarding the impact on board effectiveness of the Cadbury Committee's emphasis on the monitoring role of non-executives, while establishing his own view that 'collegiality does not have to be at the expense of effective monitoring' (Owen (1995: 16)).

It would, nevertheless, be wise to allow for the influences of perceptions and biases that beset decision-making by agents in a world of bounded rationality. As Tversky and Kahneman (1974) make clear, it is easy for rather arbitrary anchors to affect the outcomes of decisions. Specifically when non-executive directors are asked, possibly on a remuneration committee, to deliberate on the appropriate pay award for an executive, their view will be coloured by what they themselves are paid in their own companies. In O'Reilly et al. (1987) and Main, O'Reilly and Wade (1995) evidence is presented that suggests the better paid are the non-executives in their own companies, then the higher will be the pay awarded to the executive on whose board they serve as a non-executive[7].

Secondly, and no less important, by being invited onto the board as a non-executive and through the general social interplay that occurs in the course of regular board meetings, with their associated dinners and other functions, ample scope for social influence is created through notions of reciprocity, authority, similarity and liking (see Main, O'Reilly and Wade (1995: 14–20) for a fuller discussion). Many experiments regarding these effects have been conducted by social psychologists. Probably one of the more illuminating (Kunz and Woolcott (1976)) concerns the reciprocity effect that is manifested if one randomly selects 100 or so people out of the telephone book at Christmas time and then sends each of them a Christmas card, taking care to include one's name and return address. As many as 50 per cent of these strangers are found to reciprocate by sending a card in return.

Indications of these effects are found when boardroom data is examined. Thus Main, O'Reilly and Wade (1995) in two independent samples find that having been appointed to the board as a non-executive by the current incumbent CEO makes the non-executive predisposed to make a more generous pay award through the remuneration committee (by some 13 per cent of pay).

None of this should be taken to suggest that anything out of the usual or untoward is going on in the boardroom. These are simply human agents behaving in this setting much as they do in other social settings. The important lesson to be learned is that one should not expect to achieve any radical transformation of these processes simply by imposing codes of conduct. Codes of conduct will undoubtedly be observed[8], but the outcomes will continue to be subject to the type of social interaction described above. This places a premium on less discretionary and more mechanistic incentive arrangements. But as will be seen in the following section, use of some such schemes, especially share options, is heavily circumscribed by institutional regulation.

The regulatory environment – laws, rules and guidelines

While the regulatory environment covering executive pay in the USA has two major players – the Securities and Exchange Commission (SEC) and the Financial and Accounting Standards Board (FASB) – regulation in the UK is further complicated by the active participation of the financial institutions. Disclosure requirements in the UK are primarily covered by the Companies Acts (see for example Schedule 4 of the Companies Act 1989) and, where relevant, the Yellow Book Listing Rules of the London Stock Exchange (see for example LSE (1995 Amendment No.6) section 12.42(j) concerning compliance with the Cadbury Code, or section 12.42(w) which addresses the requirements of the Greenbury Code, or section 16.13 concerning the disclosure of directors' interests in company securities such as share options).

The role fulfilled by the FASB in the USA is, to some extent, discharged by the Accounting Standards Board (ASB), as witnessed by their recent ASB Urgent Issues Task Force information sheet No 10 covering the reporting of details of executive share options. In comparison with their British counterparts, both the SEC and the FASB have taken a relatively proactive stance, especially in the area of executive pay. Recently the SEC (1993) has dramatically increased the quantity and accessibility of information that must be provided to shareholders in proxy statement regarding the total pay of the top five executives in a company. FASB (1993) has recently conducted a vigorous campaign[9] to persuade companies to report and recognise employee (and executive) share options.

Where the UK seems to lead the USA is in the active role adopted by the financial institutions. This is seen in all aspects of governance but especially in the field of pay, with the Association of British Insurers (ABI, 1995), the Institutional Shareholders Committee (ISC, 1991), and the National Association of Pension Funds (NAPF, 1984, 1992) all having codes relating to the appropriate behaviour that should be expected from firms in which member institutions hold investments (and hence votes).

The prime concern of such guidelines is the protection of the investment. Thus emphasis is laid upon disclosure of details that might imply a liability on a firm to any of its directors – as in ISC (1992, section 5):

> Adequate disclosure of the principles upon which directors' emoluments are determined is essential, however, so that shareholders are made aware of performance-linked contracts and so as to ensure that in the event of a contract being terminated prematurely, any compensation for loss of office will not become a matter of contention between shareholders and remaining directors.

But most attention is reserved for the issue of executive share options where the aim seems to be two-fold: firstly to ensure that equity dilution is limited, and secondly to limit the extent to which the executive is seen to get something for nothing. Both aims are addressed in the imposition of volume caps on the issue of executive share options and in requiring performance and service hurdles on the vesting of these options. In these matters, the ABI has undoubtedly taken the lead through its 'Share Incentive Scheme Guidelines', culminating in the latest ABI (1995) version.

Over the years, in a series of revisions, there have been modifications in some aspects of the guidelines, for example in allowing new options to be issued when original grants are exercised before their full lifetime. Recently there has been a tightening in the performance hurdles that firms are now supposed to set before the executive can exercise the options (i.e., before the option grant 'vests'). But it is still possible to discern the original roots of these guidelines. They are clearly modelled upon the Inland Revenue (1984) *Explanatory Notes to the Finance Act 1984 Approved Share Option Schemes*.

It was here that the government granted a major tax concession by allowing gains from approved executive share option schemes to be taxed as capital gains (then 30 per cent) rather than as income tax (then 60 per cent for most of the individuals concerned). To qualify for Inland Revenue approval, options could last no longer than 10 years and vest no sooner than three years after issue. Issue had to be at prevailing market price and each executive was limited to holding options with cumulated exercise prices no greater than four time their current annual remuneration (effectively base plus bonus). These limitations were clearly designed to limit the tax-expenditure consequences of the concession rather than reflecting any notion of incentive alignment through the design of executive pay. The subsequent Finance Act 1988 swept away almost all of the tax advantages[10] in question by equalising income and capital gains tax rates at the margin[11].

But by 1988, the ABI guidelines had many of these parameters firmly enshrined. As mentioned above the performance criteria (or 'hurdles') have increased from the (ABI 1987: 1) requirement of 'a real growth in the company's earnings per share' to a more recent (ABI 1995: 8) 'sustained improvement in the underlying financial performance of the group in question', a condition that is backed up by several examples of explicit measures of this notion. But the 'four-times the participant's total annual remuneration' volume ceiling remains firmly in place. This is excepted for 'super options' which qualify the individual for an additional four-times tranche, but with five-year vesting and particularly stiff performance hurdles that seem to render them unattractive.

The concern of institutions over equity dilution is a valid one, and is sparked by the practice of most companies in servicing their executive share option schemes, not through the purchase of existing shares in the market place ('by acquisition'), but through the issue of new shares ('by subscription'). Egginton, Forker and Grout (1993) estimate that 79 per cent of companies follow the subscription route in spite of clear company tax advantages to acquisition. But given that current accounting practice does not require the expense of meeting executive share options through equity dilution to be reported as a charge against earnings or even as a footnote in the profit and loss account, the practice seems set to remain a common one.

Forker (1995) has examined the conceptual contradictions involved in this accounting treatment. It was a similar practice in the USA that the FASB (1993) attempted (but failed) to radically overhaul. In the UK, by contrast, the ASB (1994) recently issued a non-binding suggestion that accountants might wish to present fuller information on directors' share options so that interested parties could make their own computations regarding their true expense. This recommendation was picked up by the Greenbury Committee and appears as part of the Greenbury Code of Good Practice (Code item B5, Report paragraphs 5.13 through 5.16). But this remains a far cry from the required reporting and recognition of the expense of executive share options.

It will be argued below that this combination of circumstances has hitherto meant that the availability of executive share options as part of the design of executive pay has assumed the character of an add-on, to be supplied as an entitlement to an executive consequent on the calculation of the relevant annual emoluments (base and performance bonus etc.). Options are not regarded as an integral component of the pay package design. The remuneration committee usually takes the scope for that year's option grants to be defined in terms of the four times emoluments multiple set by the ABI guidelines and applies the formula in an automatic way, to produce option grants that are de facto entitlements rather than a calculated and considered part of an integrated compensation design. Greenbury has removed the tax advantage of executive share options (in any case modest for senior executives save as an incentive to retain rather than sell shares upon option exercise), and has rather promoted alternative long-term incentive schemes which rely more on encouraging share ownership rather than option ownership.

Were executive share options costed and reported in a more appropriate manner, then remuneration committees would be free to vary the proportion of an executive's pay that was performance related by increasing (or decreasing) the volume of share options held within an overall value of remuneration granted. Options would be seen to be 'paid for' by the executive out of forgone pay. Expressed as but one component of the overall value of that year's pay package to the executive, the incentive alignment aspect of pay would be easily achieved and subject to less of the discretionary interpretation of other more complex bonus formulae that attempt to achieve the same incentive alignment but so often seem to fall victim to the human nature of boardroom relations.

The trouble with options

The main argument being developed in this paper is that executive share options offer an attractive way of providing incentives to top executives. Valued and reported as an inherent component of pay at the time of issue, the executive can be seen to pay for any option grant out of an implicit forgone pay. The larger the proportion of the overall pay package taken up by the option component, the greater the incentive element. Most importantly, the performance-related reward or punishment impact on executive wealth will be automatically tied to the fortunes of the company and independent of any discretionary judgement of the non-executive directors or others on the board. But there are two types of objection that can be raised here. One concerns the valuation of option grants, and the other concerns their efficacy in truly aligning incentives.

The idea of pricing and reporting the value of executive share options seems a straightforward one. After all, there is an active market in share options and pricing formulae are well established[12]. Unfortunately, as Smith and Zimmerman (1976) have pointed out, executive share options are not observed as traded in the market place, and they are in some ways rather different from traded options. They have a longer life (up to ten years as opposed to nine months or so); are subject to a restriction period of three years; cannot be traded (only exercised); are subject to forfeit (for example, through job termination); and are subject to early exercise (for example, consequent upon a corporate takeover). These reservations notwithstanding, several authors[13] have illustrated that it is perfectly possible to come to a sensible valuation that factors in these various considerations, such as the inalienability of the option, early exercise due to risk aversion, and endogenous forfeiture of the option (the executive is more likely to be fired if the share price is doing badly). More worrying criticisms are levelled against the very efficacy of the incentive aspect of executive share option schemes. These criticisms generally revolve around a view that such schemes represent something for nothing, have no downside risk, can only create meaningful incentive effects if appropriately crafted performance hurdles are added, expose the executive to risk outwith his/her control, and reward the executive for general upward market movements that are nothing to do with the executive's own efforts. Greenbury (1995: para 6.28) claims that the traditional forms of executive share option 'have drawbacks' because they bring 'windfall gains' and do not lead the executive to 'build up a substantial shareholding in their companies.'

Further examples of such concerns can be found in the recent review by Conyon et al. (1995: 706–7, 712):

> ...the granting of options confers substantial increases in wealth on executives and, probably more importantly, this part will only act as an incentive if the granting of options is linked to performance.

> It is also true that, due to the volatility of share prices and the ability of the shareholder to pick the moment to sell, their initial value can be very large.

> ...potential gain is greater the more volatile the stock held and may well be unrelated to company performance.

> ...the share price appreciation of the stock option will on average reflect the general appreciation of all stocks and so a certain part will offer a gain to the holder of the option which is not specific to the performance of the firm.

Of course, the grant of executive share options does indeed have value – even at the point of issue – but if the options are 'bought' out of forgone pay, and the total pay award and its separate components (including options) are reported, then the something-for-nothing aspect is removed. It is also certainly true that volatility is a principal driver in the evaluation of share options. This can be seen in Figure 1 where the (Black-Scholes) issue value of the ABI guideline amount of executive share options (i.e., with total exercise prices of four-times emoluments) is plotted against share price volatility[14]. In each case

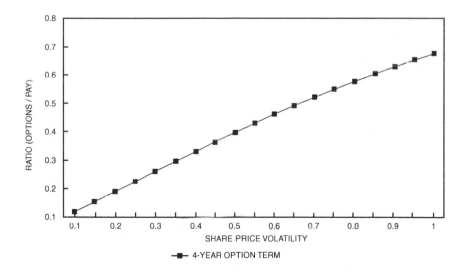

Note: The ratio is the value of the options package at issue to the PV of 4 years' pay.
Assumes a 5% discount rate and a 3% dividend yield. At £450,000 per year, 4-year PV=£1.73m.

FIGURE 1   RATIO OF OPTION GRANT VALUE TO TOTAL BASE PLUS BONUS

the assumed level of annual total cash pay is £450,000, a dividend yield of 3% per annum and a risk-free interest rate of 5% per annum are assumed. The assumed effective term of the share options is 4 years (owing to the common practice of early exercise) and the outcome is expressed as a fraction of the present value of the four years cash pay (£1.73m).

From Figure 1, it can be seen that at a typical share price volatility of 0.33, the ratio is around 0.25, i.e., the options average out at 25% of pay. With a highly volatile share, 0.65 say, the ratio rises markedly towards 0.5. A substantial amount of value is, therefore, being awarded in the form of executive share options. But unless the share price rises above the exercise price, i.e. performance is delivered, then there will be no profitable exercise of the option. However, there is an increasingly common view that an appropriate long-term incentive can only be created through the use of shares. For example the ABI (1994: 2) claims: '...some incentive should be given for part of the annual bonus payment to be invested in company shares to be held for three years or more.' And in promoting alternative share-based long term incentive schemes, Greenbury (1995: 6.32) states that 'schemes along these lines may be as effective or more so, than improved share option schemes in linking rewards to performance...' But a share option grant can create a much more levered pay-performance incentive for the same value of forgone pay.

For an executive on £450,000 per year who holds options or shares for four years in a company with a typical share price volatility of 0.33, the ABI option grant would be worth some £460,000. Under various assumptions regarding share price performance, Figure 2a demonstrates the impact on executive wealth of having £460,000 worth of options at issue versus £460,000 worth of

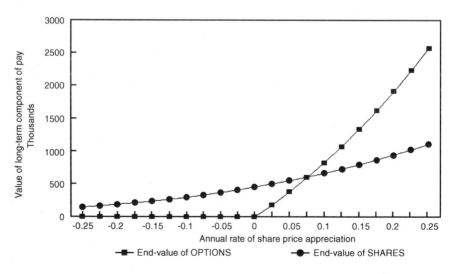

Valuation at the end of a four-year holding period.
Assumed pay=£450,000 per year.

FIGURE 2a   OPTIONS VERSUS SHARES

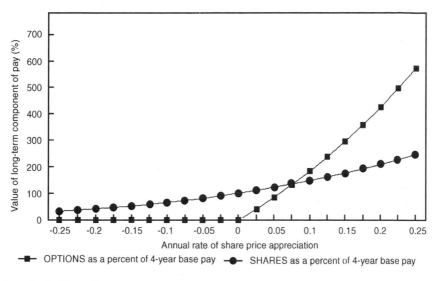

See notes to Figure 2a.
Percentage expressed on basis of annual emoluments of £450,000.

FIGURE 2b   PERCENTAGE IMPACT OF OPTIONS VERSUS SHARES

shares at issue in terms of the outturn after 4 years. The results show that the rewards to an executive for good performance rise much faster under options than shares. Figure 2b re-expresses the same result but as a fraction of annual pay (£450,000).

In terms of the benefit derived from a general upturn in market sentiment, there is an undoubted benefit to holding options. But there is a matching downside cost in a bear market, and the option will be priced to reflect these facts, and priced in terms that are available to all investors (not just insiders) to take up. Once again there is no profitable exercise unless the share price performs. The freedom to choose when to exercise the option is reflected in the pricing of the option (to the executive), and goes some way to answering the charge that the executive is holding risk over which he/she has no control, as with a reasonably long option life the executive gains some insurance against the vagaries of the market.

The fact that executive share options do indeed present the executive with downside risk can be plainly seen in Figure 3a. Here, our stereotypical executive holds either options or shares over a four year period. The yearly impact of a 5% fall in share price is shown on the market value (Black-Scholes) of the options versus the shares, until the position is liquidated at the end of year four. The option holding 'paid for' with £460,000 worth of forgone earnings can be seen to steadily become worthless. Each year the fall in value of the holding imparts a strong negative signal on the executive. Shares also fall in value, but the negative signal is much weaker with the overall portfolio losing only £85,000 rather than the entire £460,000. Figure 3b shows that with a 10%

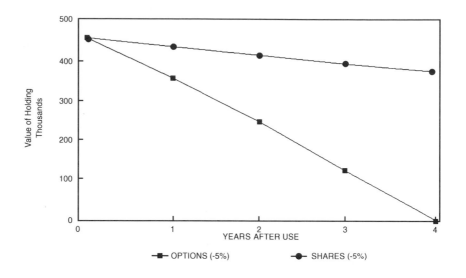

Options assumed exercised at the end of 4 years.
Calculations based on £450,000 annual salary.

FIGURE 3Aa   RISK OF OPTIONS VERSUS SHARES

share price appreciation the two modes are much closer. But at 15% the option effect is again clearly much stronger.

Placing performance hurdles on the vesting (or exercise) of options may well provide a sense of control, but stringent exercise conditions will serve to reduce the value of the option at issue and hence the price charged to the executive (or the amount of his income that he is willing to forgo to acquire this package). The executive would require a lower 'price' per option the stiffer the performance hurdles are, and might be reluctant to expose as much of his/her average earnings to such an increasingly risky prospect. Adding performance hurdles will certainly further lever the performance-reward package but, as has been seen above, even without hurdles options are highly sensitive to performance. The erection of hurdles merely introduces a needless bureaucratic complexity of administering and interpreting compliance, which renders the process subject to all the social biases discussed above. It must also be remembered that options without performance criteria are not money- making-machines, else they would be priced accordingly as we all tried to purchase them! As long as the option grant is seen as an integral part of pay, the time to apply performance criteria is when options are granted, not when they are vested or exercised.

It can therefore be seen that the use of executive share options offers a simple and potent mechanism for aligning the interests of the executive with those of the shareholder. But even if they are priced appropriately and charged as part of the overall earnings of the executive, some reservations remain. Firstly, with

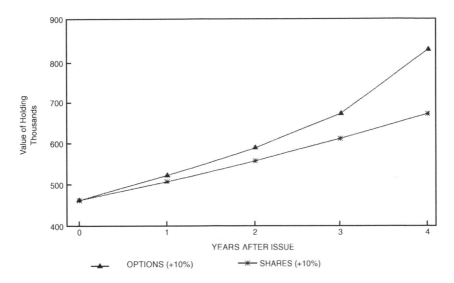

See notes to Figure 3a

FIGURE 3b   RISK OF OPTIONS VERSUS SHARES

an extensive holding of options the executive has a reduced incentive to increase dividend payouts as these may depress share prices and hence option values. Secondly, options create an incentive to the executive to adopt riskier projects than might otherwise be appropriate for the company. This owes to the role played by volatility in the option pricing formula. On the other hand, a high exposure to options in the hands of a risk averse agent may have quite the reverse influence. Either way, the risk characteristics of the company may be changed over time.

But given the current practice of share options immediately vesting in a change of control situation, it has been pointed out[15] that an underperforming management is left to enjoy the benefit of a bid premium when the market for corporate control leads to a takeover bid for the company. This is clearly a point that deserves consideration by remuneration committees when drawing up the terms of an executive share option scheme, although much as with golden parachutes there may be efficiency considerations that argue in favour of leaving matters as they are.

Conclusion

From the discussion above, it can be seen that executive share options offer an effective method on incentive alignment. They are not subject to the biases and influences that beset more discretionary and more complex performance-

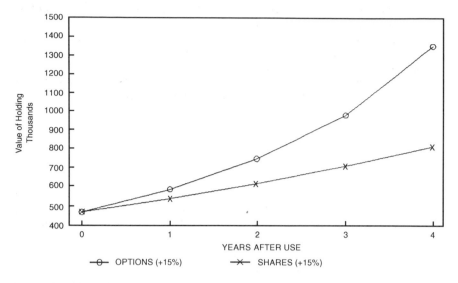

See notes to Figure 3a

FIGURE 3c   RISK OF OPTIONS VERSUS SHARES

related boardroom bonus schemes. If priced and reported in the company accounts as an integral part of executive pay, then any subsequent high reward enjoyed by an executive of a successful company is no more than could have been achieved by any outsider in purchasing a similarly levered investment in the company.

The higher the fraction of annual pay that is seen to be made in the form of options, then the more incentive oriented will be the management contract. Appropriately long vesting periods and long life terms insure both the shareholder against short-termism and the executive against the vagaries of the stock market.

The irony is that the current regulatory stance of the ABI and the general posture adopted by the Greenbury Report towards executive share options inhibits companies from adopting a more aggressive policy in terms of option grants. Some companies (e.g., Smith-Kline-Beecham) have used share appreciation rights (SARs) to emulate the properties of option grants. This seems an unnecessary complexity. But before any change in practice is possible, the accounting profession will have to confront the fact that current practice does not record the very substantial expense of executive share option awards. After Greenbury and the amendment of the London Stock Exchange Listing Rules (The Yellow Book), company annual accounts will now contain sufficient data upon which to estimate option values. But an additional step is required before remuneration committees can formulate sensible remuneration policy. The reporting and recognition of the value of option grants would be such a step. Without such reform in accounting practice, it is difficult to see institutions relaxing their guidelines.

While institutional investors share with others the desire to see executive pay become more performance related, they also see a need to resist equity dilution. If the issue of share options, and in most cases the consequent issue of shares, were accounted for as a labour expense, then this might change. But until change does occur, the connection between executive pay and company performance looks set to continue at its current generally low level.

Notes

1. There is a distinction here, of course, between a concern over the lack of pay-performance variation and a concern over the overall level of top executive pay. The latter is more difficult to address in a positive way other than to refer to measured notions of the 'going rate'. It is also much easier to muddy such considerations with overtones of greed/envy.
2. Cosh (1975) and Meeks and Whittington (1975) arc studies in the pay versus size mould. A more principal-agent perspective emerges in the case studies of Cosh and Hughes (1987) and the cross-section work in Main (1991). But it is not until the work of Conyon (1994a), Conyon and Gregg (1994), Conyon and Leech (1995), Gregg, Machin and Szymanski (1993a), Main (1992), and Smith and Szymanski (1992) that panel studies on quoted companies comparable to those in the USA are utilised. Similar work on mutuals (in this case building societies) can be found in Ingham and Thomson (1993, 1995).
3. Abell, Samuels and Cranna (1994) also highlight the impact that acquisitiveness (merger and acquisition) has on the value of executives' share options.
4. The operation of a remuneration committee in the 220 companies in the Main and Johnston sample is measured by the public disclosure of the existence of such a committee in each company's annual report. Such a measure is clearly imperfect and consequent results should be interpreted accordingly.
5. The pay of the CEO was explicitly used as an example of tournament theory in Lazear and Rosen's (1981) original formulation, and several attempts have been made to test the theory in that specific context. Lambert, Larcker and Weigelt (1993), Gibbons and Murphy (1992), Leonard (1990), Main, O'Reilly and Wade (1993), and O'Reilly, Main and Crystal (1987) present evidence for the USA which on balance offers some support for these tournament notions, although the term 'career concerns' is now more commonly used.
6. Following encouragement by the Cadbury Report, nomination committees may now be a more common and effective method of selecting non-executive directors.
7. An elasticity of around 0.1 is found for this effect.

8. Main (1993) in a series of board-level interviews with executives from 24 large British companies found that in terms of board practices and procedures scrupulous attention was paid to conforming not only with company law but also with any and all voluntary codes (ABI, ISC etc.).

9. As the SEC (1994) news release makes clear, their campaign has met with fierce opposition that looks like defeating or at least emasculating the original SEC (1993) exposure draft proposals.

10. Some advantage remains, for example in being able to make use of the capital gains tax annual exemption (currently £5,800) and being able to defer any tax liability until sale of the underlying shares rather than at exercise of the options. Also, since January 1992 exercise prices at a 15 per cent discount on the market price at time of issue are permitted if the company also operates an all-employee share scheme, although such discounts are frowned upon in ABI (1995) guidelines etc.

11. The Labour Party (1994) called for the closing of the few tax advantages that remain and taxing the proceeds of share option schemes as income (at least at the point when options are exercised). Greenbury (1995) made similar recommendations. These were implemented by the Government in July 1995 with some further adjustments in the November Budget.

12. Black and Scholes (1973), Merton (1974) or Cox, Ross and Rubenstein (1979) approaches are well established. Foster, Koogler and Vickrey (1991) and Noreen and Wolfson (1981) argue that executive share options can be valued in a similar way.

13. Including Bey and Johnson (1994), Cuny and Jorion (1994), Hemmer, Matsunga and Shevlin (1994), Huddart (1994) and Mozes (1994).

14. Volatility is measured as the standard deviation of percentage share price movement.

15. This point was made by Colin Mayer at a CEPR seminar in Edinburgh, March 1995.

References

Abell, P., Samuels, J. and Cranna, M., 1994. Mergers, motivation and directors' remuneration. Centre for Economic Performance Discussion Paper No.199 (July).

Accounting Standards Board, 1994. Disclosure of Directors' Share Options. *Urgent Issues Task Force, Information Sheet No.11*, ASB, Holborn Hall, 100 Gray's Inn Road, London WC1X 8AL.

Association of British Insurers, 1995. *Share Option and Profit Sharing Incentive Scheme*. London: ABI, 51 Gresham Street, London EC2V 7HQ.

Association of British Insurers, 1994. *Long Term Remuneration for Senior Executives*. London: ABI, 51 Gresham Street, London EC2V 7HQ.

Bey, Roger P. and Johnson, Larry J., 1994. Valuation of executive stock options. College of Business Administration, University of Tulsa, (January).

Black, Fischer and Scholes, Myron, 1973. The pricing of options and corporate liabilities. *Journal of Political Economy* **81** (May/June), 637–654.

Cadbury Committee, 1992. *The Financial Aspects of Corporate Governance*. London: Professional Publishing Ltd.

Conyon, Martin J., 1994a. Corporate governance and executive compensation. University of Warwick working paper (April).

Conyon, Martin J., 1994b. Corporate governance changes in UK companies between 1988 and 1993. *Corporate Governance* 2 (2), 87–99.

Conyon, Martin, Gregg, Paul and Machin, Stephen, 1995. Taking care of business: Executive compensation in the UK. *Economic Journal* 105 (May), 704–714.

Conyon, Martin and Gregg, Paul, 1994. Pay at the top: a study of the sensitivity of chief executive remuneration to company specific shocks. *National Institute Economic Review* 3, 83–92.

Conyon, Martin J. and Leech, Dennis, 1995. Top pay, company performance and corporate governance. *Oxford Bulletin of Economic Research* 56, 229–247.

Cosh, A., 1975. The remuneration of chief executives in the United Kingdom. *Economic Journal* 85 (March), 75–94.

Cosh, A. D. and Hughes A., 1987. The anatomy of corporate control: directors, shareholders and executive remuneration in giant US and UK corporations. *Cambridge Journal of Economics* ll, 285–313.

Cox, J., Ross, S. and Rubinstein, M., 1979. Option pricing: a simplified approach. *Journal of Financial Economics* 7 (October), 229–263.

Cuny, Charles J. and Jorion, Philippe, 1994. Valuing executive share options with endogenous departure, University of California at Irvine, June.

Egginton, Don, Forker, John and Grout, Paul, 1993. Executive and employee share options: Taxation, dilution and disclosure. *Accounting and Business Research* 23 (91A), 363–372.

Financial Accounting Standards Board, 1994. FASB agrees not to require expense recognition for stock options. *FASB News ReleaseDec. 14, 1994*. FASB, Hartford, Connecticut.

Financial Accounting Standards Board, 1993. Accounting for stock-based Compensation. FASB, Hartford, Connecticut.

Forker, John, 1995. Accounting for share based remuneration: capital maintenance concepts, performance assessment and the Coase Theorem. Paper presnetedat the Britsh Accounting Association Annual Conference (April).

Foster, Taylor W., Koogler, Paul R. and Vickrey, Don, 1993. Valuation of executive stock options and the FASB proposal: An extension *The Accounting Review* 68 (1), 184–189.

Garen, John E., 1994. Executive compensation and principal-agent theory. *Journal of Political Economy* 102 (6), 1175–1199.

Gibbons, Robert and Murphy, Kevin J., 1992. Optimal incentive contracts in the presence of career concerns: Theory and evidence. *Journal of Political Economy* 100 (3), 468–505.

Gregg, Paul, Machin, Stephen and Szymanski, Stefan, 1993b. The compensation of top directors of UK companies. Paper preseented to the American Economic Association, Boston, January 1994.

Gregg, Paul, Machin, Stephen and Szymanski, Stefan, 1993a. The disappearing relationship between directors' pay and corporate performance. *British Journal of Industrial Relations* 39, 1–10.

Haubrich, Joseph G., 1994. Risk aversion, performance pay, and the principal-agent problem. *Journal of Political Economy* 102 (2), 258–276.

Hemmer, Thomas, Matsunga, Steve and Shevlin, Terry, 1994. Estimating the 'fair value' of employee stock options with early exercise. *Accounting Horizons*, (December).

Holmstrom, Bengt and Milgrom, Paul 1991. Multitask principal-agent analyses: Incentive contracts, asset ownership and job design. *Journal of Law, Economics and Organization* 7, s24-s52.

Huddart, Steven, 1994. Employee stock options. *Journal of Accounting and Economics*, **18**.

Ingham, Hilary and Thomson, Steve, 1995. Mutuality, performance and executive compensation. *Oxford Bulletin* **57** (3).

Ingham, H.C. and Thomson, R.S., 1993. Executive compensation and deregulation in financial markets: The case of UK Building Societies. *Accounting and Business Research* **23** (91A), 373–383.

Inland Revenue 1984. *Finance Act 1984. Approved Share Option Schemes. Explanatory Notes*. London: Inland Revenue.

Institute of Directors, 1995. *The Remuneration of Directors. A framework for Remuneration Committees*, Institute of Directors, 116 Pall Mall, London SW1Y 5ED

Institutional Shareholders' Committee, 1991. *The Responsibilities of Institutional Shareholders in the UK*. Institutional Shareholders' Committee, 51 Gresham Street, London EC2V 7HQ

Jensen, Michael C. and Murphy, Kevin C., 1990b. CEO Incentives – It's not how much you pay, but how. *Harvard Business Review* (May-June), 139–153.

Jensen, Michael C. and Murphy, Kevin J., 1990a. Performance pay and top-management incentives. *Journal of Political Economy* **98**, 225–264.

Kunz, P.R. and Woolcott, M., 1976. Seasons' greetings: From my status to yours. *Social Research* **5**, 269–278.

Labour Party, 1994. Five new share millionaires, News Release, 18 August. Walworth Road, London.

Lambert, Richard, Larcker, David F. and Weigelt, Keith, 1993. The structure of organizational incentives, *Administrative Science Quarterly* **38**, 438–461.

Lazear, Edward P. and Rosen, Sherwin, 1981. Rank-order tournaments as optimum labour contracts. *Journal of Political Economy* **89** (5), 841–864.

Leonard, Jonathan S., 1990. Executive pay and firm performance. *Industrial and Labor relations Review* **43** (February), 13S-29S.

Lewellen, Wilbur, 1968. *Executive Compensation in Large Industrial Corporations*. New York: National Bureau of Economic Research.

Lewellen, Wilbur G. and Huntsman, Blaine, 1970. Managerial pay and corporate performance. *American Economic Review* **60** (4), 710–720.

London Stock Exchange, 1995. *The Listing Rules (Yellow Book)*. London Stock Exchange: London EH2N 1HP.

Main, Brian G.M., 1994. The nomination process and corporate governance. a missing link?. *Corporate Governance* **2** (3),165–173.

Main, Brian G.M., 1993. Pay in the Boardroom: Practices and procedures. *Personnel Review* **22**, 1–14.

Main, Brian G.M., 1992. Top executive pay and company performance. University of Edinburgh, Department of Economics Working Paper (December).

Main, Brian G.M., 1991. Top executive pay and performance. *Managerial and Decision Economics*, **12**, 219–229.

Main, Brian, Bruce, Alistair and Buck, Trevor, 1996. Total board remuneration and company performance. *Economic Journal*, forthcoming.

Main, Brian G.M., O'Reilly, Charles A. III and Wade, James, 1993. Top executive pay: tournament or teamwork?. *Journal of Labor Economics* **11**, 606–628.

Main, Brian G.M., O'Reilly, Charles A. and Wade, James, 1995. The CEO, the board of directors, and executive compensation: economic and psychological perspectives. *Industrial and Corporate Change* **4**, 293–332.

Main, Brian G.M. and Johnston, James, 1993. Remuneration Committees and Corporate Governance. *Accounting and Business Research*. **23** (91A), 351–362.

Meeks, Geoffrey and Whittington, Geoffrey, 1975. Director's pay, growth and profitability. *Journal of Industrial Economics* **24** (1), 1–14.

Merton, R.C., 1973. Theory of rational option pricing. *Bell Journal of Economics and Management Science* **4**, 141–183.

Mozes, Haim A., 1994. Accounting for the firm's cost of employee stock options, Fordham University, Graduate School of Business Administration, (September).

Murphy, Kevin J., 1994. Executive compensation and corporate strategy at General Dynamics, Paper presented at the American Economic Association Meetings in Boston (January).

Murphy, Kevin J., 1985. Corporate performance and managerial remuneration. An empirical analysis. *Journal of Accounting and Economics* **7**, 11–42.

National Association of Pension Funds 1992. *Share Schemes – A Consultative Approach*, NAPF 12/18 Grosvenor Gardens, London SW1W 0DH

National Association of Pension Funds 1984. *Share Schemes*, NAPF 12/18 Grosvenor Gardens, London SW1W 0DH

Noreen, Eric and Wolfson, Mark, 1981. Equilibrium warrant pricing models and accounting for executive stock options. *Journal of Accounting Research* **19** (2), 384–398.

O'Reilly, Charles A. III, Main, Brian G. M. and Crystal, Graef S., 1988. CEO compensation as tournament and social comparison: a tale of two theories. *Administrative Science Quarterly* **33**, 257–274.

Owen, Geoffrey, 1994. *The Future of Britain's Boads of Directors: Two Tiers or One?* London: Board for Chartered Accountants in Business, 25pp.

Roberts, David R., 1956. A general theory of executive compensation based on statistically tested propositions. *Quarterly Journal of Economics* **70**, 270–294.

Rosen, Sherwin, 1992. Contracts and the market for executives in *Contract Economics* edited by Lars Werin and Hans Wijkander. Blackwell, Oxford, 181–211.

Securities and Exchange Commission, 1993. Securities Act Release No. 6962 and No. 7009. Securities and Exchange Commission, Washington, D.C. 20549.

Smith, Clifford W. and Zimmerman Jerold L., 1976. Valuing employee stock option plans using option pricing models. *Journal of Accounting Research*, **14**, 357–364.

Smith, Ron and Szymanski, Stefan, 1992. Executive pay and performance: the empirical importance of incentive compatibility. Birkbeck College, mimeo (September).

Tversky, A. and Kahneman, D., 1974. Judgement and uncertainty: Heuristics and biases *Science*, **185**, 1124–1131.

The Hume Papers on Public Policy

The Hume Papers on Public Policy is a quarterly journal, providing a forum for the publication of first-class research on issues relating to public policy. It is published by Edinburgh University Press and the David Hume Institute, a non-political organisation aiming to promote discourse and research on economic and legal aspects of public policy questions.

The journal is of interest to political researchers, lawyers and economists, keeping them abreast of new developments in public policy.

Past issues have included:

- Sex Equality
- Money Laundering
- Universities, Corporate Governance, Deregulation
- In Search of New Constitutions
- Scotland and the Union
- Privacy and Property
- Law on the Electronic Frontier
- Managing Doctors
- Copyright, Competition and Industrial Design

Subscription Rates

Individuals		**Institutions**		**Single Back Issues**	
UK and EC	£36	UK and EC	£72	UK and EC	£11.95
Overseas	£39.50	Overseas	£79	USA	$20
USA	$63.50	USA	$127		

☐ Please enter my subscription to
Hume Papers on Public Policy, Volume 4, 1996 (four issues a year)

☐ I enclose a cheque made payable to Edinburgh University Press Ltd
☐ Please debit my VISA/Mastercard account number

Card No._____ Expiry date _____

Name_____

Address_____

_____ Postcode/Zipcode _____

Complete and return this form with your payment to:
Journals Marketing Dept, Edinburgh University Press, 22 George Square, Edinburgh EH8 9LF,
Tel: 0131 650 4223, Fax: 0131 662 0053, Email: Kathryn.MacLean@ed.ac.uk